San Francisco

San Francisco
CITY ON GOLDEN HILLS

Herb Caen · Dong Kingman

DOUBLEDAY & COMPANY, INC. GARDEN CITY, NEW YORK

It is entirely appropriate that Dong Kingman should be my collaborator on this book, for San Francisco—the city of his heart and mine—has been spiced and enriched by the strong flavor of China ever since it came of age as a world metropolis.

From the time the cry of "Gold!" first rang out from the Western slopes, San Francisco has been known to the Chinese of the old country as Chiu-Chin-Shan ("Old Gold Hill") or, more colloquially, as Gum San, translatable either as "Land of the Golden Mountains" or "City on Golden Hills."

It is this last translation that appeals to Dong and to me, for there is still the aura of gold over the city by the bay—an amber glow over the greatest Chinatown on the American mainland, in the golden lights of the bridges, in the topaz glints of the fog that so often films the sky.

And at dusk, when the sun sinks into what the earliest settlers of all, the Indians, called "the sundown sea," and the light is refracted from thousands of skyscraper windows, then San Francisco is indeed the city on golden hills—now and forever.

HERB CAEN

ON Powell Street, one afternoon I bumped into an old schoolmate who lives in a thriving valley town. After we'd chatted of this and that, and traded lies on how young we both looked, he said in parting: "You guys down here had better watch it. Our population is over four hundred thousand, and growing every minute. One of these days we'll be more of a city than San Francisco."

I could have replied, "When you have a million people that'll still be a small town," but you don't say things like that to old schoolmates, so I merely rolled my eyes and looked frightened. Besides, his was a familiar statement that San Franciscans have been hearing for years, and a familiar misconception: people are forever trying to measure cities in terms of population, and it doesn't work.

A city is a state—of mind, of taste, of opportunity. A city is a market place—where ideas are traded, opinions clash and eternal conflict may produce eternal truths. A city is wide open—to the winds of freedom, to the bittersweet smell of success and failure, and especially to people, all kinds of people, in their endless search to find (or lose) themselves.

A city is not gauged by its length and width, but by the broadness of its vision and the height of its dreams. There are many ways to measure a city, none of them scientific or statistical.

First, it has to look like a city—and not like The City of Tomorrow that the planners keep giving us, although those are lovely enough, in their neat scale models. When those idealized drawings, with their trellises and arbors and trailing vines and pretty little people, finally come into existence they are as sterile as operating rooms; it takes generations of triumph and misery, of human dirt and random genius, to bring them to life.

San Francisco looks like a city—the ultimate, careworn battlefield where people fight their daily fights in hand-to-hand conflict, where the houses look like places where real people actually live and die, where the soul is refreshed daily with a small victory, be it only the sudden view of bay, bridge or thrusting skyscraper—or a ship bound for the Orient.

A city is a crazy paved jungle whose people, at the end of each day, have somehow made a small step ahead against terrible odds. San Francisco is such a city.

A city has to be a place where you can get everything—and do anything, or nothing. It has to be a place where you can buy a Givenchy original, or march in a picket line. Where you can step into a newsstand and buy *Le Figaro* and the *Frankfurter Allegemeine*, or into a bookstore for a book that has been banned elsewhere.

It has to be a place where you can hear Leontyne Price in *Tosca*, followed by an hour with Dizzy Gillespie, followed by *cappuccino*, followed by a jam session till dawn in an after-hours spot.

A city has to be a place where you can see old ladies riding bicycles and older ladies in limousines. Where the hotels have doormen and the bellboys can produce a bottle of Scotch at 3 A.M. Where, if the mood is upon you, you can get blinis and caviar, fisherman's spaghetti, white figs and prosciutto, a '45 Mouton Rothschild or a movie in any one of six languages. A city is where you can sign a petition, boo the Chief Justice, fish off a pier, gaze at a hippopotamus, buy a flower at the corner, or get a good hamburger or a bad girl at 4 A.M. A city is where sirens make white streaks of sound in the sky and foghorns speak in dark grays. San Francisco is such a city.

A city, to be a city, has to be part of the congeries of world-renowned places. It has to be a member of the metropolitan aristocracy—the select of the select. A city gets that way by developing its own tradition, its own personality, its uniqueness. It has to have everything that the other great cities have—facilities, accouterments, luxuries, and squalor—plus at least one ingredient that sets it apart. This can be something as incidental as the weather or the setting. It can be the pride of its people, the laughter on its streets, or the expansiveness of its outlook. What it cannot be is a formless slurb where ideas are smothered and bigotry flourishes like a weed, and where Keeping Up With the Joneses is not as important as not being mistaken for a Jones.

A city has to have a certain accessibility. Where you can step to an airline counter and fly that day to Rome or Sydney, or sail off to Hong Kong; where you hear a dozen languages in its airport and see a dozen different native costumes on its waterfront. Where the people of all the world arrive and depart in tidal flow, carrying with them the most precious baggage of all: their individuality and fresh viewpoints. A city has to be able to accept and assimilate all this without loss of poise or understanding. San Francisco is such a city.

My old schoolmate's town is indeed growing out and out in a series of supermarket satellites, and it may someday have a million people. But a city grows only out of roots that are deep in the past, not on freeways to nowhere. Tradition, unlike a housing project, is not built overnight. A city has an identity that is recognized everywhere. San Francisco is a city.

Montgomery Street leads to the financial district towers

A TRUE city refuses to sit still, to be one place and one people. There are so many San Franciscos, for example, so many San Franciscans. You walk and you talk, you look and listen, and the truth goes on dancing brightly—just beyond reach. What is *this* city? The clichés flood into mind, making their familiar patterns: the Powell Street wooden merry-go-round (and the brass ring of the cable bell); *Siciliano* fishing boats, colorful corks bobbing in the debris-laden waters of the Wharf; the sailboat (white and fluffy) against Alcatraz (dark and craggy); Coit Tower, all golden and perfect at sunset, looking like the last time I saw Parrish (Maxfield). The picture-postcard dream city of a million tourists, and, strangely and wonderfully, of close to a million residents.

IN SEARCH OF A CITY

Three-quarters of a million people—where do you find the prototype? The well-worn, shell-thin adjectives come to mind easily enough: sophisticated, urbane, worldly. The fashionably emaciated woman in the $500 Little Black Suit, with the slim legs and the even tan and the corner booth at El Prado (and a laugh that sounds suspiciously neurotic). The Montgomery Street gentleman in the Homburg, with a *pied-à-terre* on Nob Hill, a house down the Peninsula, another at Tahoe, heading for lunch at Jack's (his eyes are tired, and they sneer). Mr. and Mrs. San Francisco, stepping right out of the four-color magazine ads, the real thing, the genuine article. And they've been around—everywhere, except their own city.

You walk along Market Street and look at the San Franciscans on parade, piling into busses, bumping into each other, crowding off the curbs, darting across the intersections like water bugs on a pond. Stout, perspiring housewives, wispy of hair and panting of breath, in cloth coats that are too short, too long, too thin. Tough young boys, all leather jacket and grease, slouching along, hands defiant in tight pockets. Schoolgirls four abreast in a sweatery cloud of giggles, swimming like bait in front of a pack of sailors. The lame, the halt, the blind, and the man giving away Bible quotations, softly murmuring, "Bless you" each time a passer-by shoulders him aside. These are San Franciscans too busy to look up at Twin Peaks in all its green glory and the Ferry Building in its freeway-hidden shame, too involved in their own struggles to have heard of such restaurants as El Prado (is it a movie house?) or Jack's (a bar, maybe?).

The city—everywhere and nowhere, to each his own, to each his zone. The neon fable of Chinatown (clatter of chopsticks and clink of glass), and down the dark alleys and up the dark stairs, the tenements and the bare wooden floors, the communal bathrooms and the sweatshops (but the children: fresh-faced as flowers after a rain). The garlicky gregariousness of North Beach (pizza, dago red, whaddya-know-a-Joe—not to mention all those topless dancers), and at midnight the old men, gray under wide-brimmed anonymous hats, alone in the corners of Mike's pool hall and the old women looking down from the open windows in their tiny flats (but tomorrow they will meet in Washington Square to talk of the good days in Lucca). You don't get the picture, all you people. Why aren't you at Kan's and the Ricksha, at New Joe's and Vanessi's and Sorrento? Acting like real San Franciscans.

San Francisco: all things to all people. Sunday brunch on a Telegraph Hill deck or a hot dog at the beach. Standing in line for a midnight movie, or standing in line

California Street with Grace Cathedral atop Nob Hill (before structure completed)

for an elevator to the Top o' the Mark. Irish coffee at the Buena Vista, a beer and a leer in North Beach, or a sun bath on the Marina Green. A cold wind ruffling the wash on the line in the old back yards of Hayes Valley, a cold martini served by a butler in a Pacific Heights mansion, coffee getting cold on a mahogany desk in a Flood Building office. Pigeons in the square, squirrels in the park, queer ducks in the bushes, and perhaps a white swan to feed at the Palace of Fine Arts—little bits of a big city, impossible to glue together.

God's in his heaven—and all's right, more or less, with this best (and most West) of all possible cities in the impossible world. Even the best city is imperfect—at best. Only now and then do all the tiny pictures fall into place. But when they do, with the sharpness of sudden revelation, the city comes to life in a burst of excitement.

A place for everything, everything in its place, the perfection of finely wrought images. Three ivory-smooth Chinese children in their Sunday robes of red, playing gravely at the base of Bufano's stainless steel statue of Sun Yat-sen in St. Mary's Square. Across the street, in front of Old St. Mary's, the California Street gusts fluttering against a nun's headdress, revealing her guileless, startlingly young face. Moon over the Bay Bridge, and a young couple on an otherwise empty California cable, kissing gently in a corner while the gripman perches sidesaddle on a front bench, clanging "Here Comes the Bride"—a beatific smile on his face.

Cameos of a city in the month of May and maybe and who knows. The uniformed doorman at Elizabeth Arden's on Sutter, bowing as he opens a limousine door for the old lady who hopes against fading hope. In Laykin's jewelry salon at I. Magnin's, the idle women with more baubles than they know what to do with are pricing new baubles because they have nothing else to do. In the glow of the Palace's Garden Court long after lunch, an empty champagne bottle upside down in a frosty bucket, cigarettes burning forgotten in an ash tray, the laughter of two people in love filtering through the marble pillars—and their waiter fidgeting nearby, glancing now and then at his watch.

The Big Picture is lost forever in clouds of double-talk, the little pictures add up to everything there is. At dawn, a squirrel scampers across the Main Drive in Golden Gate Park. Pelicans swoop low through the watery valley between the Cliff House and Seal Rocks, their fishy eyes searching the black waters below. Against the dark mass of Parnassus, lights burn after midnight atop U.C.'s Medical Center, your mind's radar clearly picks up the white-clad figures hunched around the operating table. The religious zealot walks through Union Square to warn that The End Is Near—angrily brushes a pigeon off his shoulder. (A tiny pink child, for whom the end is only beginning, squats among the birds with a bag of crumbs, delighted that attention can be bought so cheaply.)

I am a camera, and sometimes the focus needs no adjusting. A clothes-hanger-thin model swinging her hatbox as she walks through Maiden Lane—and Maiden Lane without a model is a lake without a swan, a bay without a ferry. A police car bursting out of the alley alongside the Hall of Justice, Cyclops eye swimming redly, siren scratching white-hot fingers across the blackboard of the night. A Skid Road loser passed out in classic sprawl under the yellow overhead light of a Howard Street flophouse, as dead as the empty bottle beside him. The silence of 2 A.M. in Pacific Heights, Scott and Broadway, broken by a crash of cars—and, just before silence returns, thicker than ever, the unmistakable sound of hubcaps clattering down a hill, fainter and fainter. And then, far away, another siren.

Slices of a city, thin enough to see through, yet surprisingly strong. A sunny Sunday in the Sunset, the look-alike cars parked in the driveways of the look-alike houses. Sunday hanging heavy on the "guesthouses" (the San Francisco euphemism for boardinghouses), the young crew cuts in their Bermudas lounging on the stone steps, the young girls smiling up at them—a scene lacking only its title, "The Last Fraternity House." Old couples with European faces, dressed in Sunday black, walking somberly along the flat streets of the Marina—listening for the Viennese waltz that no longer is being played, figures in a faded photo curling up in the family album.

Little bits of colored glass, the moving pattern of the kaleidoscopic city. Row of openmouthed children, adenoidally watching firemen wash their big red engine on Stockton Street. Roar out of Candlestick Park under 11 P.M. blaze of light while sea gulls wheel low across the nearby freeway to the dumps, some making it to their messy mecca, others perishing under the cars—mess, dumps, Giants, slumps, on to victory. Opera House stage entrance after the symphony, musicians standing around in black gangster overcoats, carrying violins (or machine guns?). Open window in sleazy hotel on Third Street, girl's laughter and Miles Davis's trumpet in a duet that smells of sweat and old mohair chairs with grease spots where too many heads have lolled.

The best of all possible cities, plastered with trademarks. Cable car pirouetting on its turntable, taking a self-assured bow for the becamera'd tourist. Nightly eye of Alcatraz twitching nervously in a cocoon of fog, as though looking around for a way out. And a sea gull one-legged on a piling off the Embarcadero, waiting, as the city waits, for the next move in the unending game.

This is a city of magic hours. Dawn, and the sun rises out of the east with a sudden burst that dims the lights of the Bay Bridge. At noontime, the Ferry Building raises its siren's voice, stenographers group prim as schoolgirls around the base of the Mechanics Monument to eat their paper-bagged lunches, the day's first martini-on-the-rocks shimmers on a marble table in the Palace's Happy Valley. Midafternoon's gaggle of children head home, a horseman canters along the Great Highway, a golfer in Lincoln Park silhouetted against the Chinese red of the Gate Bridge. Magic hours, all.

But to me the hour that spells San Francisco most strongly comes at dusk, when the city hovers breathlessly between two lives. For an instant the day seems to stand still, as though putting off its plunge into darkness. The light becomes hazy and dreamlike, and wraiths of the past stir in the soft shadows cast by buildings that are suddenly indistinct, ageless.

Day's end, and the sun sinking to a glorious death in the West, touching fire to a hundred thousand windows. Russian Hill is a black Stonehenge against the fading crimson sky. The first street lights coming on—pale, oh so pale. Red taillights streaming homeward, luminous fish along one-way rivers of traffic, and the great searchlight coming to life atop Alcatraz—beacon on a stone ship going nowhere.

Dusk: the great city slowly letting down at the end of the day. Skyscraper windows slamming shut. Bootblacks padlocking their stands. Sidewalk flower peddlers wrapping leftovers in newspapers. Inspectors walking out of the Hall of Justice and heading home—once again, just people. At the employees' entrances to the Emporium, Macy's, City of Paris, Magnin's, hundreds of shopgirls stand all in a tired row, waiting for their men to pick them up. One by one they disappear into the oncoming cars. Some with a kiss. Some with a bone-weary "Where the hell have you been?"

A day dies in a dizzy burst of activity: commuters trotting along Third Street, cars spewing out of garages as though shot from cannon, bundle-packing women chasing cabs that flee for their lives (they're Yellow, of course), cops standing like white-capped statues in a sea of cars, busses following each other elephantlike—each window framing a not so quietly desperate face that seems to cry out for rescue. In the soft light, the Hundred Thousands being drawn home in invisible strings—home to the hearth, home to the thawing dinner; and in a thousand corridors in a thousand apartment houses the smell of cooking stealing slowly down the hallways.

Still dusk: hint of excitement in the air—the evening lies ahead, full of promise. Maybe tonight will be the night: the secretaries, trim in their little black dresses that will go anywhere, going somewhere—the bar on Montgomery Street, or just around any corner. Buzzing over bourbon, murmuring over martinis, sly glances over the scotch, and the unquenchable excitement of the oldest game being played by a new team. It is all spelled out invisibly in the dusk that crawls out of the ocean and over the city: on to dinner with the perfumed girl, on to dancing, on to the intertwined fingers, the nuzzled neck, and let the hangovers fall where they may.

A city's past: it seems to sleep, well hidden, under the hard light of day. It is only when the street lamps come on and the cables rattle past (dimly lit, as though

by gaslight) that the long, dead nights fairly clamor to live again. Izzy Gomez, Poppa Coppa, Amelio Pacini, Halsey Mainwaring—you can see all the hosts again, greeting you with the casual warmth of their casual nights. Behind drawn shades, shadowy figures move in the upstairs dining rooms at Jack's, at Blanco's, at the St. Germaine, where the duck is being pressed and the champagne iced as the laughter rises. Already the mysterious buzzers are beginning to ring at Tessie Wall's and Jessie Hayman's, for darkness is falling over the city where history, among other things, has always been made at night.

And suddenly, in the twinkling of a sigh, it is all over—for the dusk is a fragile thing. Now the sun is far below the rim of the sea, and the last lingering traces of red and gold, of malachite and purple incandescence, have faded from the western sky. Coit Tower stands stark white against the sky, the East Bay lights glitter against velvet, a ship steals across an inky Bay—and it is too late, too late. Dusk's moments have stolen away, the moments when you make or break your evening, your enchantment, your life. Or maybe you were one of the lucky ones who made your move before the spell was broken. . . .

The pageant of the night begins with relative dignity.

The neighborhood movies fill slowly with the people from next door and around the corner. The taverns out in the avenues come to life as the couples desert their cramped apartments for a drink with their neighbors, and the atmosphere is almost as clubby as an English pub. In Chinatown's "Fish Alley," ancient yellow-skinned men gather under cruelly bright lights in tiny shops to play mah-jongg; in "Little Italy" the *paesani,* fierce of breath and mustache, begin their nightly games of bocce ball.

Flying squads of the Police Department fan out across the city in their purposefully nondescript automobiles—out into the Mission to look for car thieves, along the streets of "Little Harlem" with its marijuana pushers, through the dark and dusty Western Addition to watch for housebreakers. In the Tenderloin joints of Mason and Taylor and Eddy and Turk the sailors perch warily on stools, their eyes darting from ankle to ankle, and the lone girls, the "sea gulls," patrol Market Street, their eyes sparkly as soda water.

For some the night is as day; work is work, no matter when you do it. Irritable in the wet fog, the traffic cops swing their arms to keep warm, and along Powell the flower vendors turn up their collars, shivering at the job of selling the products of sun and heat. To each customer who complains about his weak drink the bartender complains about his flat feet, and the waiters lug their trays between the crowded tables and wish they'd decided to be shoe salesmen, instead. And cabdrivers look dismally through their flick-flacking windshield wipers and think about home and a warm bed and mentally curse the conventioneers who ask, "Hey, cabby, where can a guy find a gal in this town?"

On the Skid Road of Howard and Mission the beggars shuffle off as though they had someplace to go, some choice between starving and freezing. The pitch for "A dime fer a cuppacoffee" changes, by rote, to "A quarter for a place to sleep, mister?"—and how can you say no, even though you know both the dime and the

Market Street towards Twin Peaks

quarter will go for the same thing: a swallow of cheap wine that brings a momentary warmth at least.

Around midnight the nocturne begins to take shape. Now there is a semisilence in the air, for the theaters are almost empty, the bowlers have packed their shoes away, the bridge games have broken up (along with a marriage or two), and the night is left to its rightful and wrongful heirs. In the saloons the tempo is quickened, for only an hour or two remain to get the job done. Deserted suddenly are the streets of Chinatown, and dimly lit Waverly Place becomes the setting for a tong war in shadow play. Along the Embarcadero the great ships sleep at the ends of their lines, moving ever so slightly, as in a dream.

To the counterpoint of whimpering foghorns drama flashes suddenly in the night, jutting up here and there over the city in tiny spurts that die almost as they are born. Now, in the half-world of postmidnight, you know things are going on. In an ordinary-looking house in the Richmond District—a poker game with the stakes in the thousands, played by men whose faces are in police files all over the country. In a handsome white home in the Lakeside District—an abortion. In a Nob Hill hotel suite—a state official risking his career for a couple of champagne hours with a call girl. And in a hundred midtown apartment houses and hotels, where the lights flash on and off behind drawn shades at regular intervals, and the taxicabs come and go as though on a schedule.

Then the cavalcade goes into its last, long phase. Bandleaders, bartenders, girls head for the late restaurants, glad their work is over, but in no hurry to call it a night; sleep begins at dawn. A lone "owl" streetcar rattles along Market, forlorn, decrepit, and listing. The big neon signs have gone cold and dead, and there is no longer competition for the filigree tracery of the bridges.

The night rules with black finality over the residential districts, over Pacific Heights and St. Francis Wood, where the silence is so thick you can hear it. Soon the only lights are those high in the financial district skyscrapers, where janitresses finish their preparations for the coming day. Garbage collectors, fresh from sleep, begin hauling away yesterday's debris, singing loud Italian songs and rattling their tin cans with the assurance of those who know their jobs are secure—who else would want them? Then the first faint smudge appears in the sky behind the East Bay hills, and in a moment the night disappears in thin, cold air.

Sad, in a sense, that the night has gone. A city never quite goes to sleep. The city born with the soul of a harridan was more herself as the street lights flicked up on her hills and in her valleys. The night becomes her. Suddenly there were implications of melodrama in the blackness of the bay, splotched here and there by amber reflections from the bridges. Sharply one heard the sighing of water among the rotting timbers of the piers that bite, a row of jagged teeth, into the harbor. The cable slots sang more loudly along the quiet streets, and the fog drifted in and out of alleys, turning them into stage sets for a play that lost its actors.

The hours of a metropolis: silence and forgetfulness at midnight, peace at dawn, the morning's bright earnestness, and the fading (of spirits, energy, arches) of the afternoon. It is only at dusk, with the city turning pink and gold and shining over ice cubes, that we all start from scratch—young and headstrong again, ready for anything.

The common denominator of housing in San Francisco is a view. With the sweeping expanse of hills, harbor, and bay stretching for miles outside his window, the man in his tiny wooden house on a hill is as rich, scenically, as the millionaire in his twelve-room apartment next door. And he is infinitely richer than the well-off burgher in his St. Francis Wood mansion, whose windows can't even see around the next corner.

The San Franciscan never tires of looking at the face of his city. Thousands of them prefer to walk to work every morning, so they can gaze anew at the sights that never seem to be quite the same two days in a row. There is always a stray strand of fog across the sun to cast a new light over the rambling hills; there is always the Pacific tang to put a new bounce into your steps; there seems always to be the little inviting byway you failed somehow to notice yesterday.

But especially at home the San Franciscan wants to keep looking. He never sees enough of it. If he has a few extra dollars to spend, he is likely to invest in a larger window, or in a deck he can step onto with a visitor and say, with the smug assurance of one who is unfolding certified wonders, "Look! Where else can you see anything like *that*?"

I, for instance, once lived in a little three-room apartment on the "poorman's" side of Nob Hill. It wasn't the most convenient place in town. The wayward elevator's motions were almost as horizontal as vertical, and every time it started, the whole building shook. My rooms were as small as large closets—and there weren't any closets.

It had only one thing—a huge, plate-glass living-room window, and that was enough. For my window framed a city.

On a clear day I could look off to the left and see Alcatraz floating motionless behind a pane, and far around to the right, the valley of the financial district, where the tall buildings grow. Before me stretched Chinatown's flatness—chow-meingling around the edges with North Beach—and I could reflect comfortably that people

From Russian to Telegraph Hill, Treasure Island and the Bay Bridge

from lands a world apart are neighbors here, and good ones. The Ferry Building was my grandfather's clock—and late at night, when the darkness drew a shade over my window, I could hear the ship's bell down at the waterfront clanging out 4 A.M.

I could see a world of transportation from my window, for the bridge was arranged neatly across the middle of it, like a million-dollar ornament built expressly to be admired by my guests. Beneath the Bridge the last two ferryboats shuttled endlessly back and forth on invisible tracks. Across their white wake cut black freighters, going slowly and sullenly about their business. Between them all danced the bright sails of the tiny yachts, lighter than fluff.

History marched outside that window, for when the sun cocked a red eyebrow over the rim of the Oakland hills at 5 A.M., there was a silence of the ages over the magnificent scene; in the dim light the metropolis lost its identity. Telegraph Hill was just a blob to the left, and for all you knew Coit Tower was once again the semaphore signaling ships into the bay. There were still shadows at play in the canyon of California Street, where Ralston the Banker and Sharon the Senator wrestled for an empire—and it could have been 1929 in the lighted office high atop the Russ Building (inside sits a broken broker, looking from his ledger to the window and back again). That dark figure shuffling through Waverly Place must be Fung Jing Toy—"Little Pete"—or one of his hatchet men.

I could see other people from my window. The accordion and salami makers of Columbus Avenue, busily manufacturing music for the ears and dissonance for the

breath. The youngest generation of Chinatown, playing baseball in the alleys, where the smell of opium once hovered like a rotting flower. The impatient passengers, tumbling out of their seats to help the aged Sacramento Street bus climb Nob Hill. And the oldsters of North Beach, sitting out the twilight of their lives in the sunlight of Washington Square.

I could see the fog venturing in like an unwelcome guest. First, with an apologetic shrug, it wraps its mantle around Alcatraz, as though to say: "Well, you won't miss seeing *this*, anyway." Soon it is drawn irresistibly to the whiteness of Coit Tower, first toying daintily with it, then suddenly gobbling it whole before your very eyes. Nurtured by this solid meal, the fog lunges at the Golden Gateway complex, obliterating its mass with obvious relish, and then slides into the bay, slithering onto the bridge and gobbling its succulent orange lights one by one. Then, fatter than a well-fed python, our monster from the sea settles down to sleep, and the city must sleep with it.

I could see odds and ends of a civilization from my window. Sun bathers, stretched out on the flatness of an apartment-house roof, every line in every body straining toward the thin, wind-cut sun. Flower boxes on window sills, always the most poignant gesture of the city dweller who yearns for a piece of land. The shabby grayness of the Hall of Justice, looking no more imposing than the dregs who pleaded for humanity there. The forest of bare flagpoles atop a dozen office buildings, waiting for the holiday—or the death—that will make them blossom. The tiny one-man shops of Kearny Street—bottom rungs of a financial structure that gets bigger

From Telegraph Hill: The Embarcadero, with Alcatraz and the hills of Marin beyond, Treasure Island at right

and bulkier as it climbs toward the top. (It reaches the top just one block away, its foundations resting on filled-in land.)

These were some of the things I could see from my window—sitting in one world and looking out on another. The heart of a city—under glass.

It is raining, and suddenly the city is old, showing every one of the 1001 nights it has frittered away every year for a hundred-odd years of climbing hills, putting on frills and ducking down back alleys for a quick one—preferably after hours.

Rain, and the city huddles on its many corners, staring down at its reflection, reflecting on its yesterdays. The city seems more itself in a downpour: not quite so brash, not trying quite so hard to be as young as it will never be again. The rain is warm. It softens the outlines of buildings that are too new, too straight, too resolutely modern. It is the old gray eminences—the St. Francis, the Ferry Building, the Flood Building, the City Hall—that look at home in a city that is essentially gray, gray as the fog, the Rock, the bay, and the hair of those who love it best.

It is raining, and the Embarcadero is leaden; its piers deserted, gray, ghostly. Dark day becomes darker night; the bridge is almost invisible in the haze, like a mirage, a wild dream (no bridge will ever be built over that expanse of water). The time could be any time, and as a knife edge of moon slices through the clouds, spilling silver across the water, you could almost swear you saw a ferryboat ducking around Goat Island toward Oakland, kicking up a fine foamy wake.

Cable-car city in the rain, chained to the past with wispy memories that always turn out to be, surprisingly, strong as steel, tugging as hard as the cables under the slotted streets. On a gray day they spring back to life, as though waiting for the rain to revive them. Down Telegraph Hill they troop, down the hill that had no tower, only a semaphore, and a castle, and a two-car cable system (the one coming down the hill pulling the other up). And the great ladies that a city knew and loved, walking proudly along, their hair piled high, gardenias at their bosom, a new world at their feet: Tessie Fair, Aimee Crocker, Adelina Patti, Jersey Lily Langtry, Duse, and Bernhardt. Oh, and of course that crazy Lillie Coit, wearing her fireman's hat.

You walk over to the fireplace and look into the flames, remembering the tales Julia Altrocchi used to tell. Of Aimee Crocker's party for Oscar Wilde—the same Oscar who once toasted Lily Langtry as "Lily of love, pure and inviolate, tower of ivory, red rose of fire" (who pours out words like that any longer?). Only, at Aimee's party, Oscar was more than poetic—he was unendurable. By midnight he had drunk everyone under the table, by 2 A.M. he had switched from whiskey to gin, by 3 A.M. he was bellowing his witticisms at an empty room. Oscar Wilde, reading his poetry to San Franciscans who found him a bore. Lily Langtry, arriving here as a lady of substance should: in a private railroad car, with seven servants and 32 trunks of clothes. And Eleanor Martin, the undoubted leader of society, giving parties of such a monumental dullness that "the guests looked like they'd been frozen in for the winter."

You smile and look out at the rain that must have fallen on them all as they made their imperishable way through a city's springtime.

Crackle of log, flicker of memory—and is the city more wicked now than it was then? The ladies' daringly low-cut gowns were a scandal eighty years ago. "Low and beholds," the wits called them. "Nudity covered by transparency," scolded a critic. Said Elizabeth Cady Stanton severely: "Our fashions come mainly from the courtesans of Paris." She was reminded of the time Benjamin Franklin attended a ball in Paris, when knighthood and cleavages were in flower. "Did you ever see anything like it?" a Frenchman proudly asked. "Not," said Honest Ben, "since I was weaned."

The universality of the rain, the continuity of a city—fluid, running from generation to generation. Recently we have had the beatniks, but I wonder what they called poet Joaquin Miller, who was in the habit of arriving at the toniest parties wearing a red flannel shirt and work pants tucked into high boots. Sometimes he'd carry a pocketful of rose leaves, to strew in the hostess's path. And what of Willis Polk, Gelett Burgess, and Bruce Porter? They became so outraged at an offensive statue that stood at California and Market—a cast-iron effigy of a doctor specializing in patent medicines—that, one alcoholic midnight, they looped ropes around it and toppled it from its pedestal. The city applauded their active criticism.

The old characters of the old town: did they really have that splendid a time, or is it only because the rain is coming down, blurring everything? But there was Mayor Jimmy Rolph, coming from a party to a night meeting at the City Hall, still wearing his white tie and tails, his silver flask making a slight bulge. There were

Jimmy Phelan, Charlie Fair, and young Major Ed Bowes, the first to race their autos through the park. And there we all were at the Orpheum, drinking the beer served by waiters right at your seat.

A gray day, and memories shining through the rain. Then the skies lighten and one by one they vanish across the hills.

It's just a matter of time.

One of these not-so-fine mornings, San Francisco will wake up and discover that the manic-progressives of public transportation have finally achieved their secret ambition. There will be a strange new silence in the air. The slotted streets will seem uncomfortably quiet. And the people will look at each other in sudden consternation and gasp: "The cable cars—our cable cars—they've taken them away!"

It's inevitable—as inevitable as that bridges should replace ferryboats and that busses should supplant streetcars. Once there were a dozen cable-car lines in San Francisco. Now there are three, attacked from all sides by those clear-eyed thinkers who point out righteously that the cables lose money—while closing those clear eyes to the fact that the hinky-dinkies are worth millions annually in publicity, good will, and the kind of unique color that is disappearing all too fast from this "different" city.

So, while there still is time, let's take a ride on a Powell Street cable. Not the last ride, to be sure, but closer to the last ride than I care to think. For, as I was saying, it's just a matter of time.

The conductor sings out: "Fares, please, fares . . . Wanna transfer? . . . No, lady, you shouldn't stand on the outside step. . . . 'Board!"

Wonderful, the way the gripman climbs aboard the Powell cable after it has been swung around on the turntable, with all hands helping. The passengers are clinging to the steps and the seats, awaiting the magic moment, and then he strides majestically to the grips—like a pilot climbing into his airliner . . . And there's always the tourist staring in slight disbelief from the sidewalk by the Bank of America, while a native knowingly points out the grip and the slot and dispenses clouds of misinformation ("That gizmo there goes down through the gimmick and grabs the dingbat, you follow me?") . . . The women tuck their skirts under their legs, the gripman clangs a final warning clang-clang, and we're off past the corner sidewalk stand whose proud address is No. 1 Powell.

("Let 'em through, let 'em through . . . Plenty of room inside, don't shove . . . That's right, lady, you can transfer to the bus at Geary" . . .)

There's something open, aboveboard, and pleasantly small-townish about a cable car . . . You can smell the food being cooked in Moar's and Bernstein's and Omar Khayyam's. You can wave, Main Street style, as you bounce past saloon-keepers and florists and suit salesmen, mixing with the broken-nosers and gamblers and town characters who give Powell Street its Runyonesque flavor. You can stare smack into a hotel lobby, where a lounger sits and stares right back at you.

Then there's the St. Francis's distinguished doorman, blowing his taxi whistle in the middle of the street and almost getting clipped as you rattle past. Gray Line busses, loading up with sightseers who look out of their windows at their first strange sight—you on a cable car. You turn and glance inside the car at the people sitting behind the glass doors. You don't see anybody you recognize—and you reflect for a second on the old tale that these aren't real people who sit inside on a cable car, they're built in at the factory.

("Coming out, let 'em out!. . . Give that lady a hand with the baby . . . Awright, fasten your safety belts, we're going up . . . Whatzat? Nnno, buddy, no flight insurance on *this* trip." . . .)

San Francisco State's Downtown Center—its campus a slanty sidewalk where the students stand, one leg longer than the other, puff cigarettes and flip the butts at the slot . . . Sears, of tiny pancake fame, and The Family, a club with its prim row of clipped trees starting with precision at one boundary of its property and marching to the other—you count them as you roll by . . . And always, the intriguing windows of apartment houses passing right in front of your nose, making you a Peeping Tom whether you like it or not, and you're afraid you do, a little. The welcome plateaus of Bush and Pine, where the phalanxes of autos, four abreast, stop respectfully because they know that a cable car can't; they don't need that automatic signal to tell them that the immovable object is coming with irresistible force, and a bell to match. The gripman playfully raps out the rhythm of "California, Here I Come," and you're at—

("California Street . . . Fairmont, Top o' the Mark . . . Transfer to the Cal cable . . . How many transfers do you *want,* lady?")

One of the nicer things about a cable car is that everybody helps drive it. When it pauses for a double-parked auto, the passengers on the lower step lean out, survey the clearance with gimlet eyes, and coach: "O.K., O.K., yer gonna make it—all clear." Then the slow dip down the far slope of Nob Hill, the smart apartment houses melting into not-so-smart ones, the French laundries and the Chinese, and a snifter of garlic from nearby North Beach at Jackson, where the conductors get off to throw the hand switch and then leap back on as the car rattles, with the verve of a roller coaster, around the famed " 'Kout-fer-da-curve!" turn . . . Jackson Street, with its minor miracle of two slots and three rails so that two cars can use it by sharing the middle rail—and suddenly you " 'Kout!" again, this time into Mason Street, and you notice the dead rails of long-dead cable lines, indecently buried under pavement that covers its steel bones only in patches.

("Yeah, we stop near Fisherman's Wharf, Mister . . . Huh? Sure, you can come back on the Hyde Street line—just a couple of blocks over . . . Awright, here we go, over the top." . . .)

At Vallejo Street, you suddenly nose into space and then start down—frighteningly, fast at first, until the grip takes hold. Ahead, the bay and the stacks of steamers nuzzling up to the piers near Fisherman's Wharf . . . The big, raw hill near Green Street, with its hundreds of wooden steps going up and up while the tourists follow them with their eyes as far as they can, and then stop, out of breath . . . The swing

Powell Street lined by St. Francis Hotel, left; Union Square, right

31

into Columbus Avenue at Mason, where, for a block, you'll find four streetcar tracks, just like Market used to be; past the big night clubs and the little bars, and then the flat home stretch along Taylor Street and the final, slow clang onto "the forgotten turntable" at the corner of Bay.

The grizzled gripman takes off his gloves, leans on his lever, and grunts: "Me? I been running one of these things for thirty years. Started out on the old Castro line, ran into the Mission. Great, those Mission people. Why, the women used to jump on and off while we were running, with their arms full of babies and bundles. Yeah— I was on the Pacific Heights run, too. Women sure are different out there. Useta get sore if you didn't let 'em off right at their doorstep. What'll I do if they take these cable cars off? I know what I'll do. I'll get out of the transportation business!"

The city, which has survived earthquakes, fires, and bootleg gin to march triumphantly into a New Order of Jack Tar Hotels, concrete blockhouses and fallout shelters-cum-swinging pools, has also entered a new phase in thinking about itself. A spate of painful self-appraisal has set in. It's almost like growing up contrary to the laws of nature. Can delayed maturity follow the premature senility that came on the heels of an extended adolescence? It would seem so.

Oddly enough, as this atmosphere of self-doubt rises from the hills like a mist, San Francisco stands as an unrivaled object in the eyes of the Western world. At any given moment there is at least one writer-photographer team in town, preparing their piece on San Francisco for a national magazine, and I suppose we should be flattered at all the attention. Look flattered. Color yourself blushing pink.

But what is there left to say? After all, this is a tiny city of some forty-four to fifty square miles, depending on which magazine you read, and every square inch therein has been scrutinized sociologically, architecturally, archaeologically and illogically. At least once a week the phone rings, and there's a guy from some learned

Foot of Market Street: Freeway and Bay Bridge in the distance

journal of minuscule circulation announcing, as though for the first time, "I'm here to do a piece on San Francisco. Like to talk to you." The temptation to say, "Go scrutinize" is getting painfully strong. And then there are the photographers, poor devils. Each one is looking for "a fresh angle." That is, "I don't want to do the bridges or the hills or the cable cars; they've been done a million times. I want to capture the real *feel* of the city."

Don't get me wrong, I have nothing but sympathy for these fellow toilers in this overworked vineyard. They are handed assignments ranging from "Everybody's Favorite City" to "The Myth of San Francisco," and they are expected to make their copy sing-sing-sing without referring to the aforementioned bridges, hills, or cable cars.

I can see them now, standing hangdog at their editors' desks, while Ye Ed, tilting back in his chair, hands behind head, pulls on his pipe and says, "Nobody's really captured San Francisco yet—the indefinable charm, the mysterious life forces, the rich juices that flesh out its meager bones. I want you to explore this basic American phenomenon in depth, but keep it short. You should be able to wrap it up in three days. And stay out of the expensive restaurants." I will insert here the cynical words of one editor, for the record and the glory of reporting: "Why not? It jumps hell out of our circulation. San Franciscans love to read about themselves. And you can turn any lousy photographer loose in that town and he'll come back with something." At least we're photogenic, in the dying days before the high-rise apartments close off the last best views on earth.

The editor is right, for more reasons than he suspects. San Franciscans do like to read about themselves, but now it's more for reassurance than for the warm glow that comes from a deserved pat on the head. The old spirit isn't quite as cocky as it used to be. Once San Francisco took adoration in stride—the beautiful girl with poise. Now the wrinkles are showing—you can fool the world, but not yourself—and there are anxious looks in the mirror.

The magazines have made a fetish of San Francisco, and then accuse San Francisco of fetishism. "San Franciscans are self-conscious," they report, and go on to describe us in terms that would make Jayne Mansfield self-conscious. Our women wear basic black while doing the dishes and the men wear three-button suits with vests in the shower, for fear some magazine writer might be peeping through the window, ready to tell the world that "San Franciscans, once so prideful of their appearance, are letting down," from which they develop the theme that the whole city is letting down. Just the other day, at Fifth and Market, I saw a horn-rimmed-glasses young man making check marks on a large and efficient clipboard. Turned out he was from a fashion magazine. "I'm counting the number of women's slacks on Market Street," he said severely, making another check.

For the benefit of visiting magazine writers at the end of their expense account and close to deadline and desperation, I have prepared the following handy guide from which anybody can write a deucedly clever piece:

The Average San Franciscan: He is smug, complacent, drunk, homosexual, suicidal, has been married several times (mainly to women), lives in Millbrae, and hates his neighbors and bigotry.

The San Francisco Woman: She is vain, clothes-conscious, a social climber, hangs out in low bars, wears slacks and high heels, and has two and a half children, all of whom go to private school, except the half, who goes half a day only. She hates her husband and intolerance.

Inside Politics: San Francisco is run by its labor leaders, who are millionaires, and its millionaires, who got that way by fraternizing with labor leaders. It is also run by the Burlingame Club, the Marine Improvement Association and the Parkside Flower Club. The Mayor is a tool of the interests, which are, of course, vested.

Food: The city has a lot of fine restaurants because San Franciscans like to dine out, except those who stay at home, where they sit on the floor by candlelight and eat such typically Western fare as spaghetti and toasted French bread while listening to Bartók and reading aloud in Sanskrit. The best San Francisco restaurants are no better than those in New York and are listed monthly in *Holiday.* The food in Chinatown is not authentic except for the chop suey.

The Culture Scene: The symphony is on the skids, having been defeated three times by the Houston Colts, but is making a strong comeback under Joltin' Joe Krips. The opera, like a lot of other things, is imported and expensive. Touring ballet companies don't play San Francisco because the Opera House is used for musical comedies. However, all San Franciscans play an instrument, and every night you can hear Beethoven quartets from Hunters Point to Sea Cliff.

Put these all together and what have you got? Next month's exclusive article on "The San Francisco Nobody Knows," on the newsstands *now!*

Whenever I feel I'm getting out of touch with the city—a fear that haunts all newsmen—I take a long walk along Market Street. This is better therapy than a hot oil rub, picking up a twenty-four-point bridge hand, or flipping a cigarette butt at a cable car slot and watching it go in without touching the sides.

A few minutes on Market will convince anybody, even the oldest native, that he'll never get to know San Francisco. It's the street of broken dreams, of frozen screams, of strangers rubbing elbows—a main street a million miles away from the San Francisco the Convention & Visitors Bureau tries so desperately to portray in its magazine ads: the Tony Bennett city of tiny cable cars climbing to the stars that look down on seven-course dinners, nights at the opera, and all that sort of kitchy-koo.

In many ways Market is the most sophisticated street in town, if by sophistication you mean weary, worldly, and aloof. Its warmth is its coldness: you're alone, but so is everybody else. In a city that in too many ways is like a small town, it is blessedly impersonal. You can walk from Sixth to the Ferry without seeing anyone even vaguely familiar, and a foolish friendly smile gets exactly what it deserves: a darting glance on the edge of suspicion.

Ferry Building and Bay Bridge become part of overall view from Top o' the Mark

Market is teeming with San Franciscans you'll never get to know. It is quite clear that they don't want to know you, either. Nothing is given, nothing is expected—a truly civilized arrangement.

Market Street is the city in all its desperate vitality and glorious vulgarity—the Alcatraz of streets. It's there, but nobody knows what to do with it. Every traffic plan runs up against it and falls back, defeated. The dreamers talk vaguely of pedestrian malls and islands of shrubbery, but there is doubt even in the pretty drawings; they will end up in the files (or the wastebasket) along with a thousand other plans bravely titled, "What to Do About Market Street." It is wide, long, stubborn, and unregenerate—a true brute of a street. A dead end with a life all its own.

La Dolce Vita—"*The Sweet Life*"—a remarkable motion picture with a remarkably ironic title. The sweet life of despair, of lost people in the chic trappings of the highest civilization. . . .

But (go on, say it) it's only a movie. And an Italian one, at that. You know how the Italians are. Incurably romantic, scaling the emotional Alps and plunging, the next instant, into the wine-dark seas. Besides, the director, Signor Fellini, was being damnably clever, piling contrast on contrast, twisting life into a mocking caricature. Real life isn't that way, not life in San Francisco, at any rate. . . .

The camera rises high above the crowd, its great, impersonal eye gazing down on Market Street. An old man with a long white beard—a famine-struck Santa Claus—is walking from trash can to trash can, raising each lid and peering inside like a French chef sniffing the stewpots. (Medium-long shot.) "What are you looking for, old man?" (Close-up) "I don't know." Eyes far away, gazing at Twin Peaks. "People throw away good things, sometimes. Once I found a lady's purse with ten bucks in it." (Camera dollies up.) "Peace," reads the cardboard sign in the battered black hat of the old man on the corner; he is handing out Bible tracts, free, that nobody wants. "God bless you," he says now and then. Pickets shuffle back and forth in front of department stores. They look bored, not militant. "Nudes!" hollers the theater marquee. (Close-up of ladies in G-strings under fly-specked glass, pan to pimply young men slowly scratching themselves, follow them as they go next door to munch reflectively on foot-long hot dogs dripping with mustard.) "Vietnam!" cries the latest headline. The newsboy, a transistor radio to his ear, shakes his head. The Giants are losing. "How are the Reds doing?" Won another.

La Dolce Vita—sports cars careening down a midnight road, a man smothered by the love of a girl he doesn't want, a wild party ending at dawn to the sound of church bells, all the artful contrivings of the cinema. . . .

The camera climbs above the fog and cocks its head. On Broadway, the tourists are stacked twenty deep outside the place where men dress like women and sing bawdy songs. (Close-up of girl with hand over mouth.) "I just don't believe they're men." (Pan to her boy friend, wearing knowing look.) "You can tell by their hands and feet. Ever see any girls with hands and feet like that?" (Quick cut to a police raid on a café at Taylor and Bush.) The Mayor is pleased. "Something is being done!" Nothing is being done: the fashionable Ones don't give themselves away by wearing women's clothes or hanging out in Known bars: they wear elegant clothes, smell of expensive cologne, live at good addresses, and are left alone; an unwritten law protects leading citizens who are merely Odd. The only moral, if it's a question of morals: Don't be a poor One. Don't be a poor anything.

La Dolce Vita—Christ dangling from a helicopter, a TV crew trying to focus on the Virgin Mary, an old man going off with a tart supplied by his son . . . (Location shot: Trader Vic's.) The very social young couple is giving a big dinner party for their friends. The camera records the beautiful people: well boned, well bred, well drunk. The host signs the tab with a flourish, adding a large tip. He will pay the bill, eventually, with a check that will bounce almost immediately. He knows it. Vic knows it. It's part of *La Dolce Vita*, and anyway, his parents will make good—in the unhurried, disdainful manner of the rich. (Location shot: crowded Powell Street cable. Close-up grinning delegate, wearing name plate, "Joe.") "Boy, this is a kick. I've always wanted to ride one of these things. Great?" The little man jammed next to him nods and beams. "Welcome to San Francisco!" (Camera moves in as, with one hand, he examines the delegate's nameplate, with the other deftly extracts the delegate's wallet.) "Nob Hill!" calls out the gripman. Top o' the easy mark. (Camera pans to a black limousine parked outside the Fairmont, concentrates on the official gold seal on the doors, filmed over by the 2 A.M. fog. Its owner—not you, dear sleeping citizen—is upstairs in Room 7—. He is not sleeping. Neither is the girl.) "I can't stay all night," she is saying sleepily as the camera explores the room, voyeur-like. "I got baby-sitter problems." The sweet life has its dull realities.

La Dolce Vita—hungry hyenas with flashbulbs, suicide of a burned-out intellectual, the infinitely sad orgy . . . (The camera moves faster now, piling up montages for future editing.) "Oh, the town isn't as closed as all that," the friendly cabby is saying in front of the St. Francis. "They have girls at the—," naming a well-known hotel nearby. On Union Street, a noted art dealer lights a string of firecrackers and throws them into the sleeping street. He knows the cops will come, and they do. Anything for a laugh. "Have a drink, fellas." "No, thanks, just quiet down." Now it is dawn on Mission Street, and an old man with a beard—another old man with a beard—is dozing in a niche alongside a garage. His dirty black coat is draped around him like a robe. (The camera moves in on the empty wine bottle in his lap.) He looks peaceful. In the distance, foghorns.

La Dolce Vita—the monster that is all of us washed upon a shore, the sweet-faced innocence that is all of us calling from a great distance, unheard. But it's only a movie. Some people are even bored by it. Or are they afraid to look at themselves and the sweet life?

Down Hyde Street to Fisherman's Wharf. Aquatic Park, left

In the sudden rush to wear sackcloth instead of Dior, *nothing* is above criticism, and the critics all have a point. Market Street is too dirty (and too wide?) which rather overlooks the fact that people, even San Franciscans, are dirty. Proposed bridges are destroyed before the ink is dry on the drawing board. The busses are too crowded, the cables are too old, and the one-way streets run the wrong way. Prices are too high (where aren't they?), the restaurants aren't as good as they used to be (what is?), the people don't dress as smartly as they once did (or they overdress), and the opera company does too much Italian and not enough German (or vice versa). Old parking lots should be torn up for new buildings, new buildings should be torn down for parks, freeways should be built underground, subways should rise, and the hamburgers are too thin and the bread is too thick. Tear down the Palace of Fine Arts, restore the Palace of Fine Arts, the Palace Hotel doesn't have a sommelier any longer, and as for the symphony. . . . There are some people around who'll say right out loud that L–s A––––s isn't all that bad. After all, we have smog too, now, and what the hell are we doing about it?

As the original Glad Boy, I'm first to admit that this is not the most perfect of all possible cities. But the worst it can get, as somebody once observed, is better than any other in a world pocked with problems undreamed of. Our problems are not ours exclusively. They are those of a civilization on fire: overcrowding, inflation, an eroding brutalization of values, intolerance, a deadening conformity—and a withering of the San Francisco spirit inflicted by those (not always outsiders) whose souls are dead to the poetry of a city. To them, a tree is something to be torn down, a hill is something to level, a view is something to block, and a tradition is something they'll start themselves, at the cost of older, gentler, wiser ones.

The dangers are rippling all about us, as clearly as the flag atop the Telephone Building. Although it is slowly drying up, Skid Road is now being seen for the first time for the disgrace it is. (Once it was thought of as colorful. When a tourist would say, "This is worse than Port Said," the San Franciscan would answer, secretly pleased, "Really?") As for the Negro, San Francisco has faced the issue as shiftily as the rest of the world; where now is the vaunted reputation for freedom "as fresh as the Western wind"? The persecution of an innocent Sunset District couple by racist hoodlums could happen anywhere—but it shouldn't happen in San Francisco, "the sole emporium of a new world." Words, words, words . . .

Conformity creeps over the city like a yellowish cloud. Once, Norton was emperor and the individualist was king—the more individual the better. The city's unique character grew out of its characters. Now you talk the way I do and walk the way I do and dress the way I do or I'll turn you in. Can you imagine Harry Bridges and a shipowner debating today at the Civic Auditorium, as they did in 1936? Noncomformity today is wearing brown socks with black shoes.

In the face of all this—re-enter the Glad Boy—the miracle is that San Francisco retains so much of its flavor. The horses still canter through Golden Gate Park, the eucalyptuses still smell wetly sweet in the Presidio, the cables still clatter and clang across California and Powell, ships still go bump in the night of the fog. There is yet time. . . .

Like good health, like freedom, like life itself, do we tend to take San Francisco for granted? The well-known artist, visiting from another city, seemed to think so. He was sitting at the Buena Vista during the slow April sunset, sipping an Irish coffee and gazing out at Alcatraz, just across the watery alley. However, Alcatraz wasn't on his mind, although, like all first-time visitors, he was fascinated and his eyes kept flicking at it.

"I've been to all the great cities of the world," he said, "and not one of them has what this one has—and I'm not talking about hills or water. I mean light—fantastic changes of light. I've never seen a city move so fast or so often from gray to white to blue to pink to gold, and then back again, and sometimes all at the same time. Wherever you turn there seems to be a new shade in a new connotation—a violet hill, a yellow street, or a green house turning orange right before your eyes."

He took another sip of coffee, staring over the rim at Alcatraz, where the purple ice plant was slowly turning dark and then dead as the sun faded. As we walked outside, the city, which, an instant before, had been the enchanted pink and white of fairy tales, softened into a dusty mauve, pierced at random by the first emerging lights of evening.

The artist shook his head and looked up Hyde Street at a star hovering on the crest, blotted out suddenly by the familiar perky bulk of a cable car. "It's too much," he said slowly, "too much."

Innocence and wonderment, tinged with a slight disbelief—he was experiencing the heady intoxication we all felt once, when our eyes were new and we felt the special kinship of the specially blessed. Then, in an age that now sometimes seems as remote as the Pleistocene, we could lift our eyes above the headlines to the towers soaring on the hills. We could ignore the dust and debris of Market Street and fasten our enthralled gaze on the ornately decorated lampposts—did any city have posts as fine as these? We could look beyond the first boxlike apartments—little dreaming how fast they would reproduce their appalling kind—and see instead the delicate little Willis Polk house sandwiched between them and looking more placidly at home than their upstart, sun-blocking neighbors. We didn't need a visiting New York architect to tell us then (as he did recently) that our city hall is "the most beautiful public building in America," but his words reminded us that we've been taking that for granted, too.

The feeling of wonder—how to keep it alive and kicking strenuously. One day the ferries are on the bay, adding their unique zest to the joy of being a San Franciscan; next day they're gone, and the only sense of wonder the people feel is to wonder dully where they went and should they have done something they didn't do? One day the Ferry Building is there, a beacon lighting the golden years at the foot of Market, and the next day it's blotted out by the Embomination Freeway. When the wonder is gone, soft parks become the hard roofs of garages, irreplaceable landmarks disappear to make room for glassy-eyed monsters with the personality of robots, and bulldozers churn up the roots of poplars where Robert Louis Stevenson once sat.

Rub the years from your eyes and look again, before it is too late. Look at

City Hall. New fountain and U.N. flags in foreground

Market Street rolling grandly up to the green hills of Twin Peaks, look at Berkeley close enough to touch on a startlingly clear day, look at the fog stealing down Pacific Street as though searching for the ghost of the Barbary Coast—or Izzy Gomez.

Look at the hydrangeas tumbling down the Lombard hill and the rhododendrons reaching out to the statue of Uncle John McLaren in Golden Gate Park— and be impressed all over again at a vast aircraft carrier moving slowly along the waterfront, right at the foot of your street. The wonder is all about you even if you hardly see it any longer.

Smell the coffee hanging thick enough to stir in the moist morning air along Java Row, sniff the perennial spices where Folsom dips under the Bay Bridge approaches, and never pass a sidewalk flower stand without inhaling deeply and appreciatively—for there'd be no perfume in the air without them.

And don't wonder when the next cable car is coming along. Wonder, instead, that, wonder of wonders, there still are cable cars to come along—on tracks that one day will lead to oblivion.

You take the substance, I'll take the shadow—sometimes. In the case of a special city like San Francisco, maybe the dream is more important than the reality; it is, after all, among the most romantic of places, and what does it matter that we're no longer sure about the color of our true love's hair?

On Montgomery Street, I saw two gentlemen wearing real Chesterfield over-coats—velvet collars and all—swinging their tightly furled umbrellas with military jauntiness, and I began thinking that maybe all isn't lost after all. They cut fine figures, a sort of idealized picture of what you want men of finance to look like.

So perhaps you *can* go home again, back to the dreams of youth and the days of innocence, when all the Really San Francisco men wore Homburgs and dawdled long over fine lunches, swishing the chablis around in their goblets, and all the ladies were swathed in chiffon, had sun-tanned legs of an impossible perfection, and danced the nights away in the Peacock Court.

It must have been a dream. How else account for the fact that a full moon seemed to be beaming down nightly on a bay of lake-like placidity, while sparkling ferryboats sailed to and from the real (awful) world, out there somewhere beyond our enchanted hills?

The trouble with living long with a lady you love is that pretty soon you start seeing the pouches underneath the eyes instead of the twinkle still in them. Same with a city: it doesn't do to count the cracks in the picture window while ignoring the matchless view outside—the crazy panorama of pinnacles and pizza parlors, peaks and panhandlers, houses clinging to hills and hills clinging to clanging cable cars.

It is the very richness of the view, argues artist Frank Ashley, that keeps those cracks in the picture window from being repaired. "The problems just never seem urgent in this city," he says. "When you can look outside at the marvelous scenery, nothing else seems as important. The view overwhelms everything, even when it's disappearing. Maybe if we didn't have it, we'd get a lot of other things done."

Perhaps so, but there is still plenty of it left—more per capita than any other city in the land (in New York they're paying $400,000, for penthouses that over-look a trickle called the East River, but of course there's a forest of skyscrapers to soothe your stony soul).

Sometimes it's nice to act young and wide-eyed again. To look at the majestic symmetry of City Hall without thinking about the bumblers at work under that perfect dome (but there are some good men there, you know, some *damn* good men). To revel in the marble halls of the Opera House without looking at the patches on the great golden curtain or stewing about the criminal neglect. To gaze from Telegraph Hill at the golden clusters of the Bay Bridge, reflected on the black bay, and push aside the thought that this wonder of the world, this short-term miracle, is approaching obsolescence.

The selective eye, that's the ticket, and if you can see "an upthrusting buoyancy" in the Hartford Building and "a carousel-like gaiety" about the Jack Tar (I quote), so much the better. In North Beach, ignore the honky-tonks and consider the pulsating life, turn your back on the unkempt and smile at the kempt, the true bohemians: Wing the artist, Macchiarini the jeweler, Ferlinghetti the poet, Henri Lenoir and his magic beret, Tommy and Terry (these are ladies, gentlemen) running the parking lot next to Enrico's.

Even Market Street has its rewards. Lift your eyes from the filth and the flotsam and behold the blandishments: the young ladies with their coiffures pumped to forty pounds of pressure, the young men with ten pounds of bangs, wearing pants so tight their eyeballs bulge. The self-anointed evangelists, standing on "Nut Island" (the concrete platform at the foot of Powell) exhorting the pagans to re-pent, while the pagans shake their heads and giggle at each other, munching on ice cream sandwiches from Woolworth's.

It's hard to stay angry at a city you love, even when it does mean, stupid, or foolish things. There is still so much laughter in the air, still so much beauty in the streets; if you look closely at even the dingiest, most ramshackle Victorian house, you find a touch of style, a dusty trace of something lovely. Certainly the "new" Hall of Justice is a warehouse, but inside you bump into an old-time deputy sheriff with a friendly red face who confides, "I sure miss the old hall—it was so close to Tadich's, and man, how I loved to eat there."

It's still that kind of a city—a bit fat in the middle, a touch overfed, perhaps too fond of the good life, but still a joy. All you have to do is look at it with love in your eyes, even if it means squinting a little.

I ALWAYS suffer a bad attack of the nostalgics at the end of a year, along with the usual seasonal ailment. "It must have been something I ate," people say greenly in late December, when it's obvious that nobody could eat that many olives or pearl onions. ("Avoid painful hangovers," my friend Kenny Burt is forever advising. "Stay drunk.")

Nostalgia is more of a crying than a laughing matter. The people of this city are perennially on the verge of tears for a past that never existed except in somebody else's imagination, and at each year's end the holiday atmosphere brings it out in especially virulent form.

The city, which is losing landmarks faster than committees can be formed to save them, looks quite a bit like its old self during the great holidays. The midnight crowds around Grace Cathedral, trees shining in windows, cars double-parked outside the cocktail parties in the big houses, convivial crowds on the streets—all add up to an opulence we like to associate with the city of '49er gold and Comstock silver although it seems to me I saw an unusual number of windows without trees in one recent year. ("The trouble with a recession," as Eddie Schwartz says, "is that it always comes at a bad time.")

Strolling on Telegraph Hill, I'm especially susceptible to maudlin nostalgics. When the winds of yesteryear are right, the bridge disappears, the old orange Key Route ferries dot the Bay, and I can hear Wallace Irwin reciting his "Telygraft Hill" to a laughing Ralph Stackpole as Ralph chips away at a statue in his back yard. Then the vision clears and there is nothing really there that bites into the past except the Belt Line's tiny toy railroad—how has *that* escaped destruction all these years?— and the Ferry Building's tower, aglow with memories that bless and burn.

Among the plans for a park at the foot of Market Street is one that calls for the destruction of the Ferry Building tower. This is rich, as our fathers used to say. There's been a sort of halfhearted campaign going on to tear down the Embarcadero Freeway because it blocks the Ferry tower. Now they talk about tearing down the tower and leaving the freeway so we can have a more attractive plan for a park to commemorate an era of which the tower is the only survivor. It could happen only in San Francisco?

I am tired of Very Big Men in the Community who put a fatherly hand on my shoulder and say "Don't be a knocker, be a booster. Build things up, boy." I've had so many fatherly hands on my shoulder I'm getting all stooped over like this:). Formerly I stood like this: /, which wasn't much better, but some.

When I first put the rap on Candlestick Park, about twenty-nine minutes after it opened, a Big Man who has something to do with that Cave of the Winds said, fatherly-like: "Son, why don't you stop mentioning the wind?" "If I do," I said, "will it go away?" "That's funny," he said, scowling, "but be realistic. The park is *here*. We're stuck with it. Whaddya want us to do, tear it down?" "That's a great idea," I said, "but you haven't got the guts." "That is true," he said, chasing his hat down a ramp.

Since that day, early in '60, everybody has been blasting Candlestick, and there's just a chance that something might be done. For instance, that $55,000 wind study

Ferry Building, cut from Market Street by Freeway overpass

THE
VERTICAL
EARTH-
QUAKE

(talk about blowing money!). Maybe the experts will find a way to increase the wind enough to blow the park over Hunters Point, where they can turn it into a parking lot for Haile Selassie's yacht, or something even more useful.

When I first ventured the suggestion that the Jack Tar Hotel is slightly less felicitous than the Petit Trianon, a Big Man in the City Hall shook his head and my shoulder. "You're not showing the San Francisco spirit," he said severely. "These people are spending a lot of money in our city, and anyway, you're beating a dead horse. The hotel is here and it's up, isn't it?"

I didn't think his dead-horse allusion was especially apt, since the Jack Tar is a very live horse any way you look at it. All I know is that a lot of architectural critics and planners have expressed their opinions lately, too, about this kind of design, and that at least one builder of concrete outhouses has scrapped his earlier plans in favor of something more in keeping with the city.

I realize that nostalgia is a fairly unpopular sentiment these days, along with peace, good will, compassion, and a few other foolish notions that could get a man hauled up by a congressional committee. The cant has become a chant: you can't look back, you must move ahead, and things are better than ever. Perhaps. One improvement is that more people than ever are concerned with preserving some of the flavor and continuity of a city loved around the world for its quality and style. We know from the evidence that there was something special about the old town, but the evidence that remains is being frittered away with frightening speed.

Exactly where do you draw the line? (As somebody said, "It's a good thing the Seattle Fair wasn't held in San Francisco. If it had been, the Space Needle would've been torn down by now for a parking lot.") Nobody put up much of a fight to save the Montgomery Block, and now the architectural historians are beginning to lament the passing of this "legitimate and invaluable example of a flourishing era." On the other hand, I don't think the Fox, despite its occasional usefulness, will be missed; the theater was a legitimate example of nothing except go-for-baroque, which is what everybody did shortly after it was opened. However, the old Hall of Justice on Kearny, which is doomed, will be wept over in years to come. It has a majesty and a certain brooding personality that makes itself felt even in its present emptiness. For all the misery that went on inside its walls, it is a romantic building.

The line, and I don't mean a mythical one, must surely be drawn at the Ferry Building. I can't think of any landmark I'd fight harder to save—and not just because it's the grandfather's clock for all of us who live on The Hill. Who cares if it's only a copy, and inexact, at that, of a tower in Spain? When it's aglow at night, its warm light shines all the way back to the earthquake (for a year after April 18, 1906, the hands of its clock remained stopped at 5:17, the time of the quake) and to its days of glory as the gateway to the enchanted city (fifty million passengers a year, a volume exceeded only by Charing Cross Station in London). We all met at the flower stand in the main lobby, we watched the silent movies while waiting for our boat, and we revered the old tower for what it was—a famous city's most famous landmark.

As I drive along the Embarcadero Freeway these days I can see our symbol of

Landmark for Bay travelers: Third Street Bridge

progress—the swinging steel ball—at work. This instrument of torture, as archaic as the iron maiden, has replaced the mystical phoenix bird that soared over a city rising from the ashes. Now the golden buildings of the fabulous rebirth have turned old and presumably worthless, and back into the ashes they collapse, one by one. On the hilltops and in the valleys, the newer-yet San Francisco is rising in a series of big boxes containing little boxes, as though a giant child were at play. The authentic giants have largely disappeared.

The heavy steel ball, dangling by cable from the end of a crane, is slung, David-like, against the concrete Goliaths, built to stand five hundred years. You'd think the Nuclear Age would have produced something more complex and sophisticated than this oversized slingshot. But it gets the job done, slowly, inexorably, banging its head against a stone wall—and winning. A triumph of brute stubbornness.

I once watched the steel ball day by day demolish the Wellman-Peck warehouse that snuggled up against the crooked elbow of the Freeway. Don't look askance: the building, while constructed like a fortress, was not remarkable. Only one part of it intrudes upon my thoughts, and that is its huge old sign, once lighted by pre-neon bulbs that spelled out "COFFEE" in letters twelve feet high.

Means nothing to you? Then you didn't know the Ferryboat Era, when the city turned its best and shiniest face toward the incoming fleets on the bay, rather than toward bridge and freeway.

51

The cry of "Bring Back the Ferries!" is being heard again, but where do you bring them back from? Of what was once the greatest ferryboat fleet in the world, only two are still to be seen, and they aren't going anywhere: the mighty *Eureka* (2300 passengers), now tied up for eternity at the foot of Hyde Street, and the *Berkeley*, downgraded to a waterfront store in Sausalito. The *San Leandro*, meanwhile, molders away in a forgotten slip.

If ferries do return, they will be the new breed—fast hydrofoils, rearing up on their stilty legs like water bugs, or small, economical launches of the type that now runs to Tiburon. The era of grandeur is long gone, drowned in the lavender past. And a generation of San Franciscans is growing up that will never know the sight of a bay latticed with the foamy wakes of ships that traveled a million miles—twenty minutes at a time.

As Lewis Mumford has pointed out, the city is growing away from its most precious asset—the bay. The new buildings, rising ever higher, are blocking out what the Filler Barons are leaving of the area's most precious heritage. You see it now as an occasional patch of blue between steel; the bridges are high, impersonal and removed—you might as well be on a freeway. Today thousands of people live at the edge of a bay they've never been on.

During the century of the ferryboats the San Franciscan was very much part of his watery heritage. Blast of whistle and slap of paddle wheel, sunlight dappling the swells, the breathless excitement of a crossing in heavy fog, even the cry of "Man overboard!"—these were all his for a few pennies. The smell of the sea was in his nostrils, the creak of pilings was a familiar sound in his ears, and the sea gulls—for long years the San Francisco symbol—wheeled and screamed overhead.

The veteran skippers, the boatmen and the lookout, straining his eyes into the gloom ahead, were heroes, the very stuff of legends and dreams. They have been replaced by toll takers. It is not an even trade.

At the peak of the ferryboat era (around 1930) you could see fifty boats on the bay at one time, churning past the Gate to Sausalito, heading toward Petaluma Creek, plying between Richmond and San Rafael, tearing up the watery way to Oakland, Berkeley, Richmond, Alameda, Vallejo. They cruised at a steady fifteen knots. Oakland to San Francisco took twenty minutes—time to look at your paper, eat what is fondly remembered as the best corned beef hash in the world (thirty cents), drink an incomparable cup of nickel coffee.

Or you could watch the black-shirted Southern Pacific deck hands polishing the brass with Brilliantshine and have your shoes shined by a uniformed bootblack wearing a celluloid collar and carrying a portable footrest. On the lower deck you could examine the Wells-Fargo express carts, loaded with trout boxes from Tahoe, bars of gold bullion from the Selby smelter, early Vacaville cherries—or the occasional big redwood box with copper handles that you later learned contained a corpse.

On a stormy day the crew would commandeer a passenger (usually a boy or girl) to demonstrate the life jackets—and if you were chosen you never forgot it. Today you may also cross the bay in twenty minutes, with luck, clutching a wheel and staring at the rear end of the car ahead. No, it is not an even trade. A bridge is only a bridge, a highway in the sky. The ferryboats were close to the foaming heart of the matter—something to love.

To the unpracticed eye all ferryboats looked pretty much alike, but you soon became a member of the *cognoscenti*. The white S.P. jobs with their majestic walking beams rocking back and forth, driving the side wheels. The slick Key Routers, powered by turboelectric engines ("Smoothest ride on the bay," they said). The pride of the Santa Fe—the two-stacked *San Pedro*. The Northwestern Pacific's "floating palace," the *Eureka*, whose three hundred feet made her the longest passenger ferry in the world when launched.

The bay became your personal world. You knew Pegleg Pete, the one-legged sea gull, and John the Chinaman, peddling his nickel peanuts. You applauded The Caruso of the Ferries, the S.P. boatman who sang operatic arias as he worked. The Lavender Man, a one-armed mute, dropped his fragrant packets in your lap. You smiled at the bridge players who dashed aboard from the Key Route trains, still holding their hands, to continue their game on the ferry crossing.

The boats themselves were ornate, a tribute to the woodworker's art, related somehow to the cable cars in style and personality—a little cranky, a bit pompous and aloof. (As Jack London said to Sam Dickson one foggy day as an outgoing ferry hooted its way past their own, "Silly old ladies! That's what they remind me of—little old Queen Victorias.") But they were filled with the dignity of the era and the excitement of approaching one of the most enchanting of cities on its own watery terms.

To a raw kid from the Sacramento Valley this was part of the magic of coming to San Francisco across a dark bay whose waters suddenly began to glow in reflected glory. Adventures marvelous to relate lay just beyond those gleaming lights, just beyond the loops where the endless streetcars rattled, squeaked, and clanged their metropolitan music.

Maybe it's true that you have to be born elsewhere to appreciate San Francisco to the full (or overflowing). Not that I'm going to put the knock on Sacramento, which has a couple of modest skyscrapers of its own and a Lower End (the Sacramento term for Skid Road), once as seamy and bottle-scarred as San Francisco's.

But Sacramento is a river town, a valley town, and its pace is inevitably slower. Even as a kid I noticed that its streetcars were smaller and less noisy than San Fran-

Early look at the Embarcadero

cisco's, and they meandered along in a dream (and there was hardly anything to clang the bell at, except maybe a stray dog).

Parks, trees, and lawns are all very fine, but it was the din of the big city that fascinated me, and Market Street, roaring out from the Ferry Building on four streetcar tracks, was definitely the noisiest main street in the world. "We're going to San Francisco" was the most exciting cry a Sacramento boy could hear.

It was quite a trip in those days. If you drove, it was an all-day expedition along the narrow, winding, two-lane road—and it was unwise to take chances on such a perilous journey: you hung a canvas waterbag over the motor-meter cap. You stopped for lunch in Vacaville, asking excitedly and endlessly "Are we out of the valley yet?" (that seemed very important). And you took a ferry across Carquinez Strait, getting out of the car for your first intoxicating whiff of real bay air. The temperature dropped and you shivered in anticipation. There was no doubt now that you were out of the valley, and Baghdad lay dead ahead.

However, I preferred a long-gone electric railroad called "The Short Line" (formally, I believe, the Sacramento Northern). Like a Toonerville Trolley, this little train rattled and swayed across the flatlands and into a truly wondrous right-of-way that knifed through East Bay back yards. Clinging to your wicker seat,

Same view, new look

you could see life all around you, inches away. Wash flapping on the line. Wives at work in their kitchens. And kids perched on wooden fences, waving as you passed.

At one point this remarkable train snaked down to the very edge of the bay, and then you knew heaven was close at hand. The gray-green waters curled close to the tracks, flecked at last with the salt and spray that spelled San Francisco. The Sacramento River was wet too, but not like this. Its waters, dark and muddy, never danced to the beat of the ocean.

"The Short Line" ended somewhere in Oakland, which meant very little more to us than Sacramento, and we dashed for a streetcar that would take us to the Mole—and from that point on the dream unfolded in a series of miracles. Blast of ferry horn (hurry!), churn of mighty paddle wheels, scream of sea gull (watch out!) ineffable smell of coffee, varnish, and hemp—and then, as you curved past Goat Island, the City aglow in the gathering dusk.

Anxiously you ticked off the landmarks, and all of them were there: the Ferry tower, Heinz's big "57," Sherwin-Williams' electrical marvel, red paint flooding the green earth, and receding blackly to flood again; Wellman's "COFFEE." And, swinging steel ball or no, there they will always be.

The new parlor game—fun for young and old alike—is called City Planning. The equipment is relatively simple and any number can play. All you need is a grid map (with numbered co-ordinates), crayons in various colors, and a dice box.

The player who wins the toss rolls the dice, locates the corresponding co-ordinates on the map, and "destroys" or "improves" that square with his crayon. If he colors a beloved landmark, he gets ten points. A theater is worth nine points. If the numbers he rolls fail to intersect, he may draw a freeway—fifteen points— between the two spots and pick up any number of points in between, depending on the buildings in his path (a pre-1906 house is worth five points, as is a restaurant where Jack London is known to have eaten).

The players may give themselves various titles—State Highway Engineer, City Architect, Eastern Capitalist, and so on—and the one who destroys the City Hall for a parking lot, with a freeway overhead, is declared the winner. To add a final note of verisimilitude, all the players are blindfolded.

City Planning, like Monopoly, is just a game—a dangerous game that San Francisco is playing every day, with great recklessness. It contains an added hazard that its inventors failed to deal with: the players are not only blindfolded, they are masked, and the masks aren't necessarily black or white. It's hard for us—the public—to tell the good guys from the bad guys, and sometimes even the players themselves aren't sure. If you want to build a thirty-three-story skyscraper on a slope on Nob Hill, are you a hero or a villain? Not too long ago the answer would have been simple. Now there is a muttering in the market place.

We were delighted or chagrined, according to our various tastes, to read one day that another twenty-story apartment house would rise on Russian Hill—in a so-called "sacred enclave," complete with ramps, walls, and the ghost of architect Willis Polk. For years the general feeling in that area has been that nobody would dare desecrate it with a towering slab of concrete. Good taste and an ingrained love for San Francisco would prevail, and so on.

Well, we learned something—again too late: traditions taken for granted are soon turned into granite. The Russian Hillers who opposed that twenty-story building expressed a deep, if not necessarily exclusive, love for San Francisco and made agonized appeals to ethics and morality. That lady who wanted to build that skyscraper probably loves San Francisco too, in her own fashion, and would like to make a buck, besides. That is also a sacred tradition.

If what's left of the physical character of San Francisco is to be preserved—like Topsy, it "jes' growed," and it accidentally grew handsome—the law has to be changed. Frank Lloyd Wright once said "San Francisco is the only city I can think of that can survive all the things you people are doing to it and still look beautiful." Then, reverting to his role of curmudgeon, he snickered that "What San Francisco really needs is another earthquake," which overlooked the fact that we are having an earthquake—a vertical one.

Changing the law to provide for zones that are indeed sacred and untouchable— for reasons of history, beauty, and just plain breathing space—is not going to be easy. There are people in the City Hall who would tear down the City Hall without a qualm in the name of that magic slogan: "Get it on the tax rolls!" And we have powerful groups who would rise in anger if a large corporation, offended at what opposition was raised, had announced, "All right, if you don't want us we'll build our building in Oakland, or Los Angeles." A high chamber of commerce official said to me: "We *want* big buildings here. We want this to remain the business capital of the West." So does everybody—as long as the buildings add to, rather than detract from or even obliterate, the surrounding areas. "Don't let that ghost-town talk start up again," warned another official. "We don't want people to say San Francisco is dying."

When can a city be said to be dying? In the journal called *Christianity and Crisis*, Howard Moody answered that question this way: "A city is dying when it has an eye for real estate values but no heart for personal values, when it has an understanding of traffic flow but no concern about the flow of human beings, when we have competence in building but little time for ethical codes, when human values are absent at the heart of the decision-making and planning and governing of a city—it is dead and all that is left is decay."

Then he quoted T. S. Eliot, in *The Rock:*

> Though you have shelters and institutions,
> Precarious lodgings while the rent is paid,
> Subsiding basements where the rat breeds
> Or sanitary dwellings with numbered doors
> Or a house a little better than your neighbors;
> When the Strangers say: "What is the meaning of this city?
> Do you huddle close together because you love each other?"
> What will you answer? "We all dwell together
> To make money from each other"? or "This is a community"?

I stood in the rain on O'Farrell Street, watching the wreckers at work on the Alcazar Theater. The marquee, which had glittered with two generations of stars, was denuded. Gone were the banner and pennants that had fluttered across the façade. In the back, a crane was chewing away, like a dinosaur in a forest of stucco and steel. A few blocks distant, the carcass of another playhouse—the State, nee California—thrust its bare ribs to the leaden sky. This one had been built like a battleship. It was dying hard.

I stared at the ugly, rain-drenched face of the Alcazar, trying to summon a lump to my throat. If I had been Edwin Booth, I might have leaped to the middle of the street to deliver an impassioned soliloquy on the death of a theater, to stop the carnage while there was still time. Of course, I didn't. Who wants to be taken for a nut? Besides, the traffic was quite heavy.

Switching sentiments in midstream of consciousness, I looked at the theater with the hard-nosed eyes of a cynic. After all, it hadn't been much of a place. The main floor was too deep and not properly canted. The acoustics: only fair. The lobby was pitifully small and a little fire-trappy in feel. As for the stage, as many flops as hits had appeared there, as many inept performances as memorable ones.

But, as I shivered there in the rain, it came to me that none of these things mattered. What mattered was that another public gathering place was going—a place where, some future day, one of the greatest shows ever seen in San Francisco *might* have been staged, a show where people would have laughed and applauded and walked out humming a song. The odds against it were long, sure. But now they're infinitely longer.

A man walked out of Bardelli's, placed a toothpick between his teeth, and stood alongside. "So they're finally tearing down the old wreck," he observed. I nodded. "Well," he went on, "I've seen plenty of lousy shows there." "Ever see any good ones?" I asked. "Oh, a couple, maybe," he conceded. "From now on," I said, "you're not going to see anything there but a few parked cars." He shrugged and started away. "That's life, buddy," he said, not unpleasantly. "You can't stand in—." "I know," I interrupted. "You can't stand in the way of progress." He gave me a funny look and walked off. Why argue. He was, after all, as right as the cold rain that was trickling off the plastic helmets of the wreckers, glistening on the flanks of the giant crane that was hard at work to make the city safe for seventy more parked cars. And eventually a "motor hotel."

Make the world safe for the caristocracy, the autocrats, the motormaniacs. I walked over to my Mission Street garage, got into my car, and inched into the glacier of chrome, glass, and rubber. I felt guilty. Here I was, grandly alone in a car that would seat five. I looked around at the big sedans alongside. One person or sometimes two, drawn by three hundred horses that could gallop at one hundred miles an hour—barely moving through the maze we had created for ourselves.

We oozed along, turning expensive gasoline into smog, past yellow zones and red, "One Way Only" and "No Left Turn," parking meters and slickered cops on tricycles, four-story garages and garages under uprooted parks, past an infinity of signs reading "Sorry—Full" and cars parked under "No Parking" signs, through a million dollars' worth of traffic signals, augmented by an army of officers waving their arms while banks were being robbed and old ladies attacked. Insanity.

I remembered a conversation long ago with a great man in City Hall. "No private cars should be allowed in the downtown area," I said. He looked shocked. "Don't you believe in the free enterprise system?" he said. "In *this* country"—as though I were from some other—"if a man can buy his own car, the fruit of his labor, he should be free to drive it anywhere he wants. Why, our free people would never stand for such a restriction."

Here we were, we free people, driving a carful of empty seats, speeding anywhere we want at five miles an hour, feeling the ulcers forming at every tangled intersection. We are the guilty, all of us. We tore down the Montgomery Block and tore up Portsmouth Square. We tore down the Alcazars and most of the other concrete links in a city's continuity. Oh, we have power, no doubt of that. We are bending, breaking and reshaping a whole city to our will and selfishness. Nobody is going to tell *us* we can't drive our battleships to work.

"But you don't really miss the Montgomery Block, do you?" a man asked me the other day. Yes, I do. It was fat and squat, but it was authentically old, by San Francisco standards, and its thick walls told silent stories of Sun Yat-sen and Mark Twain, James King of William, and Kathleen Norris, and O. P. Stidger dramatically saving it from the army dynamiters in 1906: "If you blow up this building, you'll have to blow me up with it." Now it is a parking lot. There is no poetry in a parking lot, but I am in no position to complain.

O. P. Stidger had only the United States Army to face. He didn't know that I, and an army like me, driving down Montgomery Street in our lordly cars, in a lardlike stream, would be the ones who'd destroy his beloved landmark.

Soon after that day, I was riding with a cabdriver who gunned across Fifth and Market, grazed a frightened covey of pedestrians, cut in on a truck, forced a car to the curb, and remarked to me, "They're ruining this city." He was one of the rudest drivers I've ever been marooned with—a true anarchist of the traffic wars—but it is always "they" who were at fault.

And so it goes, the livelong day. Why don't "they" do something about civil rights demonstrators, freeways, high-risers, and teen-agers? I've seen teen-agers and the motorcycle gangs stop on the highway to change flat tires for old ladies—the same ones who cluck-cluck about "teen-age punks" and "what is this world coming to?"

It's not "they" who are responsible for what pains or delights us about the city and our life in it. It's us. Anarchy is a strong word, but it begins at home; if you define it as a breakdown in law and order—and a disregard for your fellow man—there's plenty of it around. There's a little anarchy in all of us who complain about freeways and insist on driving our cars to work; let the other guy take the bus. There is a touch of anarchy in the pedestrian who walks against the "wait" signal, and plenty in the nut who runs a red light. As for the man whose new building robs thousands of their view, or levels a green hill in the sacred name of free enterprise—well, maybe that's the divine right of economic royalty.

A city, any city, is always in a state of anarchy, more or less controlled. For a city is the world—or the jungle—in microcosm, and the laws of the jungle prevail. Let me get mine, and then we'll worry about the common good. As for what constitutes "mine," it's every man for himself.

The old-timers think the newcomers are ruining the city, and the newcomers regard the old-timers as a bunch of fuddy-duddies intent only on preserving a distant dream. There are people who believe, in all honesty, that San Francisco should have as many skyscrapers as can be crowded onto the existing space, "because that's what makes New York exciting, isn't it?" What makes (or is it made?) San Francisco exciting is a unique expanse of sea, sky and hills; when that is gone, at last, this will be a Minimanhattan.

There are those who can't understand all the fuss about freeways. Young people born in the Freeway Age can't see anything wrong with a device that takes you where you're going as fast as possible—no matter how much beauty was sacrificed in the process. There is even something to be said for the Embarcadero Freeway; if affords a brief glimpse of ships at dock, something few people could see before.

As for the highway engineers, their problem is simply to build a straight line between two points at the lowest possible cost (in millions), and if something like Golden Gate Park gets in the way, too bad for Golden Gate Park. In the hierarchy of anarchy, the car is god and a place to park is heaven.

Well, there are a thousand viewpoints in the city—and a view is sacred only to him who has one and is in danger of losing it. The Negro marching in a picket line couldn't care less about the new blockhouses in the sky, and the worker who lives in the Deep Mission isn't likely to shed any tears over a freeway that nips off a corner of a park he never visits.

Albert Schlesinger, a dedicated civic leader, says that "If we had allowed the Palace of Fine Arts to disappear, San Francisco would have had a black eye all over the world"—which may be stretching it a little. It won't matter a whit in Ghana, Guiana or Genoa, or even to the man on Third Street crouched in a doorway with his bottle. However, the Palace became a symbol in the battle for beauty and tradition. Thanks or no thanks to William Howard Taft, San Francisco has been stuck with a label, "The city that knows how," and the know-how is somehow concentrated in a poetic structure that was built to fall down.

(I have the feeling that fifty years from now some savage satirist in the mold of Evelyn Waugh will write a screaming novel about a millionaire giving two million dollars for the restoration of a temporary building—only to find it is not enough by far. As war, pestilence, and famine wrack the world, the red tape grinds inexorably until at last, out of the ashes of a dead city, rises a gleaming fifty-million-dollar palace, built by the skeletal survivors to the memory of a man long dead.)

Franklin Murphy, chancellor of U.C.L.A., has said: "If we do not return beauty of the environment to a position of the highest priority, we shall have made of our growing megalopolises a major force for human brutalization." He wasn't speaking of the Palace of Fine Arts, but the words apply to what it symbolizes as a counterbalance to Neo-Box building and the strangle hold of freeways.

Brave words, Dr. Murphy's, but they are only words, and a city's people will not respond to stimuli that have no meaning for them. There will always be those who find a fifty-story building more exciting than a Palace of Fine Arts. The challenge to "the city that knows how" is to find room for both, and it's not "they" who are going to solve the problem. It's little old anarchistic us.

One night I walked and looked and thought about what I had just seen. Then I wrote:

The light is eerie at midnight along O'Farrell, in the devastation and desolation of the Western Addition. A feathery film of fog floats endlessly across the moon, and the tough old city cats prowl through the shifting shadows, picking their padded way in and out of craters, over the rubble, between the skeletal trees. There is an icy silence, as of death.

The wreckers with their swinging steel balls and their flailing axes have done their job well. For block after block, the ground has been cleared; Berlin, during World War II, looked this way after the last bomber had vanished into the west. Here and there, a house still stands—looking slightly dazed, through broken windows.

The dark side of the moon: you stand on the edge of the emptiness and try to remember all the wonders and monstrosities that stood there—the sagging wooden steps, the stoops, the stained-glass windows and the bays, the quatrefoils, the dormers, the carved pillars, all the intricate gimcracks and gewgaws of carpenters' Gothic that gave a face to a city's golden age. You poke around among the ruins, like a veteran home from the wars to find his home obliterated. A trace of foundation, the outlines of what must have once been soft green gardens surrounded by wooden fences, where people long gone sat and smiled up proudly at their ornate houses.

It doesn't much matter. Soon even these traces will be gone, buried under row upon row of concrete dormitories where life will be neat, orderly, square, efficient and electronic. New trees will be planted, looking sterile and anemic. There will be new lawn, sparse and pale. And many children, all looking oddly alike.

Midnight, in the wasteland of the Western Addition. Two blocks over, you can see the bright lights of Post Street with its jazzy joints and barbecue pits, looking like the main street of a small Western town. And farther up the hill, the soft golden haze of Pacific Heights, its big houses rich and secure: death for them is still a generation away.

At the corner of Franklin, a tall palm tree still stands, spared by the wreckers in some fit of sentimentality. Tired and old, it droops slightly over the street that once was the most stylish in town, as though mourning the mansions that died around it. And a block away, the revolving sign of the Jack Tar Hotel whirls merrily —the garish shape of things to come.

There's no use crying over spilt milk, especially when it has turned sour. San Francisco's Victorian Age is over—bad riddance to the good parquetry, the brass chandeliers, the high ceilings, the iron gates. The city, despite its desperate clutch on the past, has moved up another notch in history.

Lately, I have been looking at the old downtown apartment houses with new and sympathetic eyes. Now that so many of the boarded ancients have been destroyed, they are next in line. One by one, in the years to come, they will be tumbled down, and with them will go tumbling a whole new set of memories.

San Francisco's downtown apartments are unique in my experience. No other city has so many, clustered together in one area, looking as though they were designed by the same architect, all of a piece and era. They reek, some literally, of the Tasteless Twenties, with their decorated stucco, their ironwork doors, their tile lobbies, their fluted columns, their vaguely Spanish influence (Spanish was very big in the twenties, heaven knows why). And yet, I'll miss them, too, when they are finally gone. For the typical San Francisco apartment house has played a part in all our lives—and there will be nothing quite like it again.

If you lived in one, you lived in them all. Every man Jack among us had a girl who lived in one at some state of his love life. Rich and married lawyers kept (and still keep) their girls there. During Prohibition they housed speak-easies. After Prohibition, they contained after-hours joints. When the town was open, bookies and madams operated there. Widows, bachelors, young newlyweds, the whole Sanfrantasmagoria living cheek by jowl by howl by the skin of their teeth, trading cups of sugar (or marijuana) over the stoops, above the garbage cans in the concrete court.

The old apartment houses, all smelling alike: cabbage, even when it isn't cabbage. The elevator, creaking and swaying as it rises, with many a frightened click. The dimly lit halls with the drab, patterned carpet of indeterminate hue. The doors, each with a tiny peephole (the password was "Swordfish!"). And the apartments themselves. You could walk through each one blindfolded and never stumble across a stick of furniture, so many times have you seen it all: the mousy sofa, the easy chair with the crocheted antimacassar, the pseudo-Oriental rug, the footstool (one leg loose), the hexagonal coffee table (two burns), the slight smell of gas from the leaky stove. And the cracked plastic radio, held together with adhesive.

*Washington Street, between Montgomery and Hotaling Place, as seen in 1946
when Dong Kingman shared a studio with sculptor Pucinnelli. This was the
bohemian Montgomery Block, now Jackson Square and a decorator's center*

View of North Beach from Dong Kingman's rooftop at Dawson Place

This is San Francisco too—a big stucco slice of it, of what we were and what we are. When the bell tolls at last for the old apartments, the planners will watch the carnage unmoved, and a lot of you will say "Good riddance," as you said good riddance to the Victorians.

But where then shall we look for the vanishing roots of a city?

"San Francisco," wrote a gentleman in the New York *Times*, "is the most nostalgic of American cities."

He was, of course, making an educated guess. You can't put a yardstick on memories any more than you can measure a dream. The old-timers of Quincy, Illinois, or Cedar Rapids, Iowa, undoubtedly gaze into the past as fondly as any vintage San Franciscan, although you are entitled to wonder (as a proper San Franciscan) what they have to look back on that is half as grand as our own heritage.

". . . most nostalgic of cities"—a loose phrase, kindly but imprecise. I know a lot of young people here, and some not so young, who are hankering for more "progress," and as one who believes in storing up memories for future reference, I feel sorry.

Somehow, I can't see them, fifty years hence, sitting around over a bottle of good port and sighing "Golly, remember the old Bayshore Freeway and dear old Cemetery Curve?" Of course, I could be wrong. Maybe that's all they *will* have to talk about—these old San Franciscans of tomorrow.

Memories are a tricky commodity, and a city, like a woman, is determined to have a colorful past, no matter how much self-censorship (or self-delusion) is involved.

We remember the fun of the auto ferries and forget the one-hour wait to board one on a football weekend. ("Bring back the auto ferries," a few really dedicated nostalgics are forever suggesting, but who would ride them?) We remember the exhilarating roar of the four streetcar lines on Market, forgetting the graft, the scandals, the inefficiency, and the ever-present danger of being crushed between them. We dote on the recollection of Sunny Jim Rolph, with his carnation, his dazzling smile, his polished boots, conveniently forgetting that he could never come to grips with a problem and would be lost today. We recall the old passenger ferries, and forget the stormy, frightening days on that bay, and the collisions in the fog.

We filter our memories until only pure sunshine remains. Perhaps a psychoanalyst would say we are really groping painfully for our own youth, when we were unscarred, undefiled, perfect—godlike creatures strolling the springtime streets of our lost city. But no, I deny it. San Francisco grew strongly out of its past. It falters only when it grows away from it.

When you're in love with a city, you grope for shadows that vanish at first touch. The years lengthen, memories grow vague, even the hills change shape; you find yourself clutching at smoke rings. Harder, now, to call back to life the rattle and roar of the iron monsters, the go-to-hell brashness of a city where many a help-wanted ad might warn, "Only native San Franciscans need apply." And so you surround yourself hopefully with the yellowing, crumbling substance of the city that was—the dim photos, the ancient guides, the notes from graybeards with total recall. They write from everywhere, these old-timers—from Los Angeles, from Seattle, from the Midwest, from New York. They prove there is no such thing as an ex-San Franciscan. By their testimony, you know that no American city was ever so loved, and you try, with whatever evidence you can collect, to put your finger on a pulse that has long since ceased to pound—except in memory.

Evidence of a vanished world. I have here a 1903 menu of the Spreckels Rotisserie—a restaurant in the sky of San Francisco. It was on the fifteenth floor of the Call (or Spreckels) Building, an ornately domed, cupola-topped beauty at Third and Market. (Today it is Central Tower, a blank, unexciting shaft.) The menu is oddly romantic. On the cover is a drawing of the great building at night, its dozens of circular dome windows blazing out against a starry sky and a new moon. On the back of the menu are photos of the various views—east to the old bay-windowed

Up an old wooden stairway from waterfront to Coit Tower, Telegraph Hill

68

Washington Square, North Beach. The church is Sts. Peter and Paul, the statue the Volunteer Firemen's Monument, presented to city at bequest of Lillie Hitchcock Coit. Coit Tower to right

Palace Hotel and the sailing ships alongside the Ferry Building, north to a strangely flat Nob Hill, west to the spires of vanished churches, south to a Mission District that was the fighting heart of the city.

Inside is a picture of the Rotisserie. Like so many things about old San Francisco, it looked intensely European—pillars, potted palms, polished mahogany cabinets, huge tablecloths reaching to the floor, waiters with batwing collars, fiercely mustached men with their bosomy wives and little boys dressed inevitably in sailor suits. The menu itself indicates that the Rotisserie was no short-order, meal-a-minute house. Ten oyster dishes alone. Scotch woodcock, terrapin à la Maryland, chicken à la gouverneur, mallard, sprig, teal, and canvasback duck, *pâté de foie gras Strasbourg*, Lalla Rook, charlotte russe—and as for the prices. If I listed them you would break down and sob. I will merely record that the menu warns "No check issued less than 25¢."

Evidence of things past. I have here a 1922 booklet of the local Musicians Union. From its moldering pages rises the sound of dozens of orchestras playing in the likeliest and unlikeliest corners of a city that must have loved music, loved to dance, loved to hear a violin while dining.

Even the cafeterias had good-sized orchestras—violins, cellos, flutes, clarinets, harps, the works. The Clinton featured Marie Coletti Weiler and her Ensemble. Dave Randall and Ed Fitzpatrick fronted eight pieces at the Crystal Cafeteria. Genevra Waters Baker and her Magic Violin, backed by six good men, played at the Sunset Cafeteria No. 1 at 40 O'Farrell. The theaters had near-symphonies. Gino Severi led forty-five men at the California. The never-to-be-forgotten Paul Ash and his Synco Symphonists—all eighteen of them—were at the Granada. The Royal, the Strand, the Pantages, the Orpheum, and even the New Fillmore ("Strachan and His Orchestra!") were alive with live sound. The New Mission "proudly presented" The Incomparable Fabello and his orchestra, and where are you now, O incomparable one?

It is a staggering list to read in this jukebox age. Ballrooms—Adele Steinbeck and her L'Aiglon Orchestra, Heinz's Melody Orchestra at Maple Hall on Polk, Wallfisch's Winter Garden Jazz Band, Cy Trobbe at the Arcadia. Herman Heller led three groups at the Palace Hotel—the Rose Room Bowl Orchestra, the Concert Orchestra (twenty-one pieces) and the ten-piece Tea Room Orchestra. And let us not forget Tom S. Gerunovich and his Wilson Dance Palace Orchestra, or Norman Woodside and his "Irresistible Dance Music" at Cafe Roberts-at-the-Beach, or George Lipschultz's Music Masters at the Warfield. The Casino Theater Orchestra under S. W. Rosebrook, featured Morbid C. Pringle on trombone. Morbid C. Pringle, whoever and wherever you are, I miss you.

Evidence, drawn from the letters of those who refuse to forget. Eddie Graney's billiard palace in 1911, with the most lavish free lunch in town and the great Willie Hoppe taking on all comers and collecting all bets. As late as 1909 you could see bearded prospectors on Market Street, their guns strapped to their legs and ready to fire. At the Ferry Building, you stood in line to sign your name in "The Largest Guest Book in the World"—a five-foot-by-five-foot monster.

Tillie Belmont, a reigning madam—and what a name was that!—would serve you champagne even if you just dropped in for a chat. The poor kids of Butchertown got bladders from the slaughterhouses and blew them up into footballs. Along the streets at early dawn, boys pushed little green carts filled with fresh loaves of French bread, propping a loaf against the front door of each regular customer. And at Van Ness and Geary stood the great wooden revival Tabernacle, where Evangelist B. Fay Mills raised a bony finger to Heaven and warned of "terrible things to come!" The tabernacle is long gone. It is now the site of the Jack Tar Hotel.

Even veteran world travelers, well-seasoned in their salt-and-pepper tweeds, seem to agree that it was quite a town in the olden, golden days. "The greatest city I ever visited," one global gadabout once told me, "was San Francisco—a city that died in 1906."

Old San Francisco. "The city that was never a small town" definitely had something, and whatever it was, they still talk about it. Not in the manner of historians, with meaningless dates and esoteric anecdotes, but in an endless mumble-jumble of names and places and happenings that still seem tinged with a special kind of brightness.

"Do you remember?" the old-timer always demands. Yes, remember:

When a jockey named "Snapper" Garrison rode the great horse Boundless to an amazing victory in the '94 fair—giving birth to the term "Garrison finish." When a gang of pioneer ruffians used to shout, "Huddle 'em, huddle 'em!" as they crowded around their victims—thus coining the word "hoodlum." When a gambler who hung around the Cliff House used to challenge his fellow betters in a loud phrase that he invented to live forever: "All right, put up or shut up!"

Remember the old Orpheum on O'Farrell Street? Its regular customers held their regular seats for the gala Sunday-night performances year after year—and the ambition of every prominent San Franciscan was to get a permanent pass to the theater. One day Charles L. Ackerman, president of the Orpheum, bestowed this most princely of favors upon Horace Platt, president of the now also defunct Geary Street Railway. Platt was overjoyed until he noticed, in small letters at the bottom of the pass, the following legend: "Not good on Saturdays, Sundays, or holidays."

So he had a special Geary Street Railway pass made for Ackerman. On the bottom of the card was printed, in equally small letters: "Not good going east or west"—the only directions traveled by his company.

The old Orpheum. A lot of tears have been shed over it. When he appeared for the last time on its stage, Ted Lewis had to pull his old silk hat down over his eyes—to hide his grief. Today, there is nothing to mark its site. Perhaps the last San Franciscan to "enjoy" the Orpheum was a real estate operator named Maurice Moskovitz. Just before the wreckers went to work, he sneaked inside, found his old "permanent" chair, and sat there alone for a few minutes. Yes. He cried too.

The Tenderloin. The clean old man was lounging against a wall at Taylor and Ellis, watching the Hilton Hotel rise in all its dubious glory. "Well, that's it, kid," he said with a resigned smile. "That is the end of the Tenderloin."

Botanical Garden, Golden Gate Park

Across South Drive from the Arboretum, Japanese Tea Garden

The Park's 1017 acres include a buffalo paddock

As he spoke he was rhythmically flipping a twenty-dollar gold piece, that talisman of the old crowd. "Of course," he went on, "the Tenderloin has been dying for years. But that thing there"—he jabbed a finger at the monumental blockhouse—"that's the gravestone." He chuckled without amusement. "Sort of looks like one, too."

I glanced around. There were more parking lots and fewer places to go. Nearby, a new jewelry shop was being installed. A streamlined branch of the world's biggest bank was already in business. A small hotel once noted for all-night revels has become a "residence" for "senior citizens," that irritating euphemism.

His purple-veined face shadowed under the pearl-gray fedora, the clean old man squinted into the late-afternoon sun. Two hard-looking blondes in linty black slacks and high heels gave him a brief "Hi, baby" as they walked past. His eyes followed their rears down Ellis. "Won't see much of that any more," he said. "The old Tenderloin is about to get as square as that hotel. Now tell me about all the conventions Mr. Hilton is gonna bring to town, and I'll ask you—where they gonna go for laughs when they get here?"

The old Tenderloin—the "Terrific Triangle" bounded by Jones, O'Farrell, and Market. Tenderloin: a peculiarly American term, born in New York. The lexicographers aren't too sure about its origin; the most educated guess surmises that the cops on a certain beat in Manhattan were able to afford tenderloin steaks. In San Francisco, the juice was rich enough for filet mignons, sparkling burgundy, apartment houses, and places in the country.

In the few blocks of the Terrific Triangle, for a comparatively few years as a city's time is reckoned, there was more action than anywhere else in the country. There were fine restaurants: the Techau Tavern at 1 Powell, Newman's College Inn, the Bay City Grill, Herbert's Bachelor Grill. There were the "French" places—Blanco's, the St. Germain—with utter respectability on the ground floor, shady booths on the second, "riding academies" (as they were known) on the third.

You could drink till dawn in Dutch White's at 110 Eddy and at Chad Milligan's Sport Club on Ellis. Fanchon & Marco danced at Tait's Pavo Real on O'Farrell, where a kid named Rudolph Valentino was a bus-boy. Frank Shaw and Les Poe reigned at Coffee Dan's. It was unthinkable to miss a Sunday night at the old Orpheum, and if the bill there was a little weak (Jack Benny and Sophie Tucker), there was always the Tivoli, the Warfield, the Capitol, the Alcazar, or Will King's Casino, with Will singing "I've got a girl who paints her cheeks, another with a voice that squeaks, they both ran away with a pair of Greeks—I wish I owned a restaurant!"

Girls, girls, girls. Every theater had a line, with Stage Door Johns to match. Every other small hotel was a house (the old Drexel alone had thirty girls). A doll with the marvelously San Francisco name of Dodie Valencia was a legend. Even the manicurists at Joe Ruben's barbershop were "as beautiful as Follies girls," the supreme accolade of the era.

But the lifeblood of the old Tenderloin was gambling. The cards shuffled and the dice rattled through the smoky nights at the Menlo Club and the Kingston and at Milligan's. The high rollers—Nick the Greek, Titanic Thompson, Joe "Silver Fox" Bernstein, Eddie Sahati—faded in and out with the foggy dawns. At Tom Kyne's in Opal Place, the cul-de-sac alongside the Warfield, you could bet on anything from the Mayor's race to the St. Mary's–Santa Clara football game to how many passengers the ferries would carry next day.

The gamblers were the kings of the Tenderloin, and their names rang true, straight out of Runyon and Lardner. Carnation Willie and Benny the Gent, Bones Remmer and Siggie Rosener, Freddy the Glut, Jelly, and Marty Breslauer. At 10 A.M.—the end of the day that started at midnight—the bookies gathered at John's Grill on Ellis. Over the corned beef hash and the eggs sunnyside up they counted the cash and paid off the winners. Enough long green was scattered over the tables to carpet Ireland. Marty Breslauer alone packed $100,000, and one night a kid he'd befriended gunned him down for his roll.

But violence was rare. It was an underworld with class, a closed corporation. The cops, who were getting their share, kept it that way, and the hoods of the Organization never had a chance to move in. When they arrived at Third and Townsend they were met by the two toughest inspectors on the force, who put them right back on the train.

The cops knew a good thing, and they had it. The mother of a captain on the force was the biggest madam in the area. One day at Bay Meadows a rookie cop who didn't know the score told her: "One of these nights I'm gonna come into your place and close you down." "And when you do," she replied coolly, "you'll find your boss in the kitchen drinking coffee."

It was a world we'll never see again. Godliness and purity now reign—don't they?—and the final long shadow is being cast over the Tenderloin by the Hilton. The section is about to become infinitely more respectable. And infinitely duller.

The City That Was. Remember when all the horsecars were converted to cables —sometime in the nineties, wasn't it?—and hundreds of homeless families flocked to buy the suddenly outmoded conveyances? These they hauled out to the sand dunes near Ocean Beach to convert into homes, and overnight the "city" of Carville was born.

For years the strange community flourished. Potted geraniums flowered in the streetcar windows, and the wealthier squatters added lace curtains. Where the well-to-do of today sport two automobiles, the aristocrats of Carville owned two horse-cars, tacked together to form a single dwelling.

But Carville was doomed around 1910, when the city decided to grade the Great Highway that runs grandly along the ocean front. The horsecar forerunner of the Sunset District was condemned, and the squatters sadly gathered their pitiful baggage and trooped desolately across the sands in a new pilgrimage to poverty.

San Francisco had an especially gala Fourth of July celebration that year. As massed thousands watched from the surrounding dunes, the Fire Department destroyed Carville in a blaze that still burns in the memories of oldsters. Trumpeted the mayor as the embers glowed to death, "May San Franciscans never again be reduced to living under such miserable conditions." (Brave words those. But to-

St. Mary's Church and Square, with Bufano's twelve-foot granite and stainless steel statue of Sun Yat-sen

The blocks rise around St. Mary's Square in Chinatown. "Today the park becomes a cage." –DONG KINGMAN

day many a San Franciscan, living in a dank basement or a cold cubicle, would welcome a horsecar to call home. . . .)

The old days. Once you start dreaming, the recollections come back in clusters.

Rosetta Duncan, later to become famous playing Topsy to her sister Vivian's Eva, doing a little Dutch-boy act at John Tait's O'Farrell Street café—and quitting when he refused a five-dollar-a-week raise. The late movie comedian "Fatty" Arbuckle, showing that he had a heart somewhere in his heft by buying a new mattress for every prisoner in the county jail. Jack Warner, now one of Hollywood's powerful Warner Brothers, running a tiny theater on Fillmore Street near Sutter—and having the nightly receipts changed into nickels so he could count them out with his now forgotten partner ("one for you, one for me"). The pretty little usherette at the Castro Theater, whose name meant nothing then; a few years later every movie-goer was talking about Janet Gaynor.

The memorable night when madam Tessie Wall shot her estranged husband, Frankie Daroux, in Anna Lane—then calmly awaited arrest and later offered to save his life by donating her blood. The great fighter, Stanley Ketchel, showing up at Shreve's swank jewelry store on the morning after a successful fight, wearing a dressing gown and escorting a beautiful woman for whom he'd casually select expensive trinkets. "Dasher Jack" Cannon, the Beau Brummel of the Police Department, who always carried an ultra-thin silver-plated gun, a gift from a visiting celebrity named Rudolph Valentino, who was impressed with the officer's impeccable clothes and insisted that the ordinary service revolver caused an unsightly bulge.

The names, the faces, the places that stick in your mind! Charlie Chaplin, Gentleman Jim Corbett, and the Great Fitzsimmons, giving free shows every Sunday at the Chutes on Haight Street. The block bounded by Powell, Ellis, Mason, and Eddy containing more nationally known cafés than any other block in the country—the Louvre with its imported beers, the Oriental, Teddy Lundstet's, Shiff & Dow's, the Langam, Pratt & Tierney's, Spider Kelly's, Jack Morgan's, the Inverness, Haymarket, and the original Techau Tavern. Louis Coutard, the chef at the old Poodle Dog, proudly concocting the delicacy that still bears his name—crab Louis.

The celebrated sea lion, Ben Butler, that used to sit in front of the Cliff House and patiently shake flippers with thousands of local yokels each Sunday. And the two trained canaries that were the cutest sight to see at Sutro Baths (one of the birds would pull the lanyard of a tiny cannon, whereupon the other one would fall "dead" into a miniature coffin). The sensation of 1910: Jim Woods, manager of Hotel St. Francis, making the public pronouncement that henceforth women would be allowed to smoke in the lobby and hallways.

Colorful characters, colorful customs, colorful costumes.

And the old Palace Hotel, for decades the most elegant hostelry west of Chicago, full of history and historic incidents. Like the time President Ulysses S. Grant, on his first visit to San Francisco, received such a mighty acclaim as he drove into the rotunda that a Chinese waiter on an upper balcony leaned over to see what all the shouting was about. Only one thing was wrong with this understandable gesture: the waiter forgot that he had a tray full of dishes on top of his head. They landed squarely in the President's lap.

Around the Palace they still talk about the day a white man and his Indian wife arrived from Alaska, where he had just dug up a fortune in gold. He wanted nothing but the best, or better, so the manager installed the couple in an elegant suite on the top floor. But lo, the poor Indian wife of the rich miner was so unnerved by the elevator ride that when dinnertime came she told her husband to go ahead. She preferred to walk down to the dining room. A few minutes later she joined her husband at his table, holding a large hunting knife in her hand. Her explanation was simple: "I blaze trail down to dining room so could find way back after dinner." For six floors she had hacked chunks out of the expensive woodwork and banisters!

Yes, characters, always characters.

Memories of April 18, 1906, too, the day of the earthquakes and fires and the death of an era. They still talk about John Tait running out of his Powell Street apartment seconds before the building collapsed and dashing like a crazy man to his great café. He stood outside a few seconds and cried with relief because it was still standing. Then he unlocked the front door and walked in—to find that everything but the front wall had been demolished.

They still talk, after all these years, of tenor Enrico Caruso picking himself up from the floor after the first shock had thrown him out of bed and vowing in a loud and frightened voice, "I will never set foot in San Francisco again!" (Although, obviously, a foot was not what he was setting on San Francisco at the moment.) The little-known sequel to this gaudy fable being that he was all set for a triumphal "homecoming" concert in San Francisco some fifteen years later—only to die an untimely death in Italy.

They like to tell the story of John Barrymore, still clad in white tie and tails, wandering about the shattered city on the morning of April 18 and talking a newspaperman into sending an emergency wire for him to his uncle, John Drew, and his sister, Ethel, in New York. In the telegram John fabricated a doleful tale of being jolted out of bed, wandering around the city in a daze, and being forced by a brutal soldier to grab a shovel and work for twelve solid hours. In New York, Ethel read the wire, turned to Uncle John, and asked, "Do you believe it?" Answered Drew firmly, "Every word. It took an act of God to get him out of bed and the United States Army to put him to work!"

And, if their memories are especially good, they might smile about the opening, just after the fire, of a makeshift opera season at the Chutes Theater at Fulton and Tenth Avenue. It was *Lohengrin*, starring the hefty Mme. Lillian Nordica. During the performance she fell down a flight of stairs, shaking the stage so palpably that the whole audience rushed frantically into the street, thinking it was another earthquake.

But always, when they talk about the events of April 18, they talk about the courage of the survivors. Few tributes were more to the point than that of Major

General A. W. Greeley, the martial law administrator, who wrote: "It is safe to say that 200,000 people were brought to a state of complete destitution. Yet I never saw a woman in tears, nor heard a man whine over his losses."

It remained for a young man named Larry Harris to capture best the proud, cocky spirit of San Francisco in 1906. He did it with a poem called *The Damndest Finest Ruins*, which, I'm sorry to say, few of the city's present generation seem to have heard of.

If anybody ever gets around to drawing up a final, authenticated list of Who Did What for San Francisco, I hope the name of Alma de Bretteville Spreckels is right up at the top of the list. She and her late husband, Adolph B. Spreckels, gave the Palace of the Legion of Honor museum to the city—and I never look at this glorious building, with its Roman arch and Ionic columns, its equestrian statues and rolling lawns, and its spectacular perch on a rise overlooking the Golden Gate, without marveling at the magnitude of the gift.

The Legion of Honor is a splendid example of San Francisco's *Belle Epoque*, when fortunes were huge, purse strings were open, and nothing was too good or too expensive for a city that reveled in its own luxuriousness, a fat cat on a satin pillow. Today the very atmosphere is different for a variety of reasons, most of them plausible if depressing, and few San Franciscans give a second thought to Mrs. Spreckels and her magnificent monument.

But I hope that this lovable octogenarian dragon of a *grande dame*, up there in her baroque mansion on Washington Street, splashing in her heated pool and putting a good dent in her martini, knows that a lot of us are grateful and always will be. Even if we seldom get around to saying so.

What started me thinking about Mrs. Spreckels—and others—was the opening of a cabaret theater called On Broadway, above La Strada restaurant in North Beach. In its own, and much different, way this too is a contribution to the sometimes mystical atmosphere of San Francisco. To build it required courage and the kind of hang-the-expense attitude that belongs more to the Spreckels era than this tackier one of Think Twice, Go Slow, and then Cut Corners.

On Broadway is the concoction of Keith Rockwell, owner of the Purple Onion, and a few of his associates. They started out to convert the loft above La Strada into a theater for about $30,000, painfully scraped together. They wound up spending over $100,000, because once they got started they decided to go all the way.

On Broadway is a jewel of red carpets and red walls, with a foyer that looks out on the financial district, a mahogany bar, and good wood and good chandeliers everywhere. You can drink and smoke in your comfortable seats while the show is on, and there is even leg room. I don't know whether Keith Rockwell and his friends will sink or swim, but either way they have the satisfaction of knowing they did it in the grand manner.

I'm dwelling on these widely disparate examples—the old museum and the new theater—because they illustrate a point. San Francisco has long had a reputation for expansiveness, a kind of freewheeling, Western openhandedness, that delights in doing things up in scarlet ribbons imported from France, and this reputation is being chipped away by the merchants of shoddy. To them a view is something to sell as cheaply (to them) and as expensively (to you) as possible. A building doesn't have to be a work of art or fit into the neighborhood—it's simply a matter of cost-per-square-foot. A room doesn't have to have bookcases or fireplaces, and if a wall cracks every time you drive a nail into it—well, who needs pictures, anyway? The only thing special about San Francisco, in their eyes, is that it has too many hills that should be leveled and crowned with boxes as soon as possible, and if they could find a way to fill in the bay and cover it with shopping centers, they would. And probably will.

The old guys thought big and built well. The City Hall is a good example of extravagant nobility, and the tired old Ferry Building still has a feeling of breadth about it, a touch of dignity that even obsolescence can't destroy. The fine old houses of Pacific Heights were put together to last for generations, and they remain, triumphantly, one of our crowning glories—something the new apartment buildings will never become if they stand forever, which they won't.

The man-made objects that gave San Francisco its unique atmosphere gain in stature every year. The examples are everywhere, and every year grow more remarkable in contrast to their newer neighbors: the vast lobby of the Mills Building, the medieval bulk of Grace Cathedral, the meticulously wrought façade of the Fairmont (but not, no, never, the tower), Ignatz Steinhart's aquarium in the park, —right down to such random examples as Albert Samuels' huge street clock on Market, and the row of jeweled lamps in front of the St. Francis.

Today there is pettiness in the streets. Every man who puts a cheap and garish sign on his building is spitting in the eye of San Francisco.

But there are those who are keeping the faith. The advertising firm that converted an old Pacific Street firehouse into its handsome offices is keeping it. By preserving the last of the Bonanza Kings' mansions, the Pacific-Union Club justifies its existence. Every restaurateur who puts fresh flowers on his tables and serves his salads on cold plates and stocks a decent wine cellar is living up to the tradition. Jackson Square is a delight, and so is Enrico Banducci. Simply by inventing a hungry i, as Mr. Rockwell concocted a Purple Onion, he has kept alive the beguiling notion that there is something slightly mad about San Francisco.

He's only out to make a buck? But isn't everybody? It's just that some give more than they take. Some take away a view, others add to the vision of a city, and to them we owe more than we can ever pay.

Base of the San Francisco–Oakland Bay Bridge

The building of the Bay Bridge, completed in 1936. The painting is contemporary. "I watched it grow from the stringing of wire until the day they made it one unit." –DONG KINGMAN

From the Embarcadero, the base seen previously in close-up and the completed span to Yerba Buena Island

To some, it is a sign of weakness to look back. I had lunch one day with the late Will Irwin, and I arrived with a thick notebook and plenty of pencils, ready to bask in the reflections of the man who wrote "The City That Was." The sentimental historian of pre-firequake San Francisco was pleasant but unrewarding. "No, the city isn't what it used to be and it never was," he said, disposing of the subject. "Now that I'm an old man, I only think of the future," but he looked sad as he said it. The past he had once extolled—the old houses, the old streets, the old friends, the old restaurants whose menus he detailed so lovingly—was too painful to contemplate.

The late banker Parker Maddux, who had been a young man in old San Francisco, liked to scoff at those who sought the vicarious memory. "Why, this was just a small town then," he'd mutter over the French bread at Jack's. "What was it? A few hotels, a few restaurants, muddy streets, a dirty old Chinatown and you'd catch your death of cold on the ferries." But he wasn't convincing, sitting there fingering his thick gold watch chain, his eyes looking far back to a gentler era.

Nearby sat one of the New Breed, a hard-eyed builder of boxes on hilltops. "You can't bring back the past," he said, his fingers curled around a 6-1 martini.

Well now, there is something to be said for that attitude. It's hard, forthright, practical. And, for all I know, it's a realistic summing-up of the attitude of all the New San Franciscans, who came here—and are still coming—for any number of unromantic reasons: job opportunities, fed up with the Eastern climates, looking for a bridge to jump from, or whatever. I confess that I know very little about these newcomers and their tastes—and if their ladies like to come downtown in slacks and if their gentlemen prefer to wear sport shirts to restaurants, I'm sure only a hopeless fuddy-duddy could object. For this is the way things are in the age of the split-level, barbecue-pitted mind, and I agree it makes precious little difference to them that the Pacific-Union Club was once "Bonanza Jim" Flood's mansion, or that the old White House Department Store was founded by a Frenchman who invented a chicken dish acclaimed from here to the classic eating places of Paris.

However, I'm a hopeless fuddy-duddy. People in love—especially people in love with a city's will-o'-the-wispish spirit—can't help looking foolish. I am a hopeless nostalcoholic—a disease that afflicts all San Franciscans sooner or later, and will strike the newcomers eventually. It comes from drinking of the past, and there is no escaping it in this city where it is always present. Damn and doom me for a reactionary if you will, but I still find a cable car a more cunning piece of design than a freeway built across the graves of houses that once knew laughter and tears.

It is true, Newcomer, that I remember things I never saw, but then, all San Franciscans are born with memories. I never attended the Midwinter Fair of '94, but when I pass the glassily Victorian conservatory in Golden Gate Park, I can imagine the way it was, and see the bicycles coming in many-legged clusters down the Main Drive, and the ladies in their plumed hats, wasp-waisted and shy. I never saw the 1915 exposition, but when I stand below the Palace of Fine Arts, I can visualize its sister buildings ranged across the Marina, and the tiny mirrors of the Tower of Jewels aglow with a thousand fires, and Al Jolson and Sid Grauman and Harry Richman entertaining along the Midway. And can you pass Third and Market without remembering exactly the way it was—even if you weren't there—on the night in 1910 when Tetrazzini sang "The Last Rose of Summer" for the assembled hundred thousand? Of course you can't, if you're really a San Franciscan, for all this has been woven somehow into your fiber.

You are looking bored, Newcomer. You are worrying about the mortgage on your tract house, the tax rate, the next payment on your fast-back car, where to go on Fourth of July weekend. These are nothing. You can worry about them anywhere. As a San Franciscan, you should have more important things to worry about. You won't miss the gingerbread monstrosities of the Western Addition? But they, too, were part of the warped roof of San Francisco: bulging bay windows glinting in the sun, wooden stairs leading to the past, peaked roofs totally unsuited for a TV aerial. They weren't good for much, agreed, except that they made a city look like San Francisco.

Does the past really mean so much? The Ferry Building will disappear too one of these days and then a fresh batch of newcomers will wonder why *you're* so upset, Newcomer turned Old-timer. Is the city any less because all the renowned characters have gone forever—from Oofty-Goofty to Barney Ferguson and Tiny Armstrong? I think so. I think it's too bad that the city has grown so big and impersonal that nobody has time for the care and feeding of characters, be they bearded poets in search of the truth—whatever that is—or hopeless lunatics with a pathetic willingness to be laughed at. But then, as I said earlier, I'm a fuddy-duddy. When I hear a Chinese and a Texan in conversation, it's the Texan who sounds foreign to me.

You can't bring back the past any more than you can deny it existed—and the fact that it existed is implicit in the thoughtful buildings that have aged with a grace the new builders will never achieve, even if, by chance, they should happen to stand that long.

". . . most nostalgic of cities," wrote the man from New York, and it is possible to infer a criticism. Nostalgia—an excessive and sentimental yearning for the past. I agree it is pointless, if enjoyable, to dwell on the heroes who are long gone (would Ernie Nevers be a football star today?) and the seventy-five-cent Italian dinners with wine in North Beach (you were making only twenty-five dollars a week in those days, weren't you?) and such impossible niceties as that provided by the Occidental Hotel, whose staff used to meet incoming guests at the Oakland Mole with hampers containing fresh fruit and chilled bottles of California wine, to eat while crossing on the ferry.

A healthy regard for tradition is not a weakness. "The memory," wrote Thomas De Quincey, "is the book of judgment," and the future will judge us by what we do in the present. I hope it's half as good as what our predecessors did in the past.

On top of Stockton Street tunnel looking toward Church of Sts. Peter and Paul and North Beach area

THE city: one by one, its familiar buildings crumble away to be replaced by new ones that stare you down with glassy-eyed hostility. The hills where poppies grew (and children played) disappear under rows of houses with one-tract minds, holding hands in loneliness. Out of the slums of yesterday rise the tenements of tomorrow.

But, for better or bitter, a city is still more than sticks and stucco, bricks and bric-a-brac. A city is still more its people than anything else, children scampering home in the sunny 3 P.M. of their young days, graybeards doddering nowhere in the 3 A.M. of their eternal nights, people clinging to the sides of cables and the ghosts of the past, those who feed the pigeons and those who are fed up with them, the Beat and the Square, the foul and the fair. . . .

The city divides and subdivides, the people merge and multiply, walking crookedly along the neat white lines, jamming into busses, bustling into tall buildings, pushing trays (and each other) in cafeterias, elbowing their way into bars— but still loving life (and each other) enough to stroll hand in hand across the bridge, with no thought of jumping, thinking only of tomorrow and all the tomorrows blooming on the hills.

Unique. The city is filled with individuals leading their private lives—separated by a few inches of wall, an inch on the crowded bus, fraction of an inch on a downtown street corner. All looking alike and yet different, going in the same direction to worlds apart, living next door, but as remote as Laplanders. People who nod to each other daily, the simultaneous nod of hello and good-by. You look at them, as they look at you, guardedly, wondering who they are, what they think, how they love, where they go to do whatever they do. . . .

City of strangers you see every day. The cop on the corner you've nodded to for twenty years; suddenly it dawns on you that you've never seen him in civvies— and would you recognize him if you did? The old blind man who taps his way along Mission, wearing a wildly incongruous white crash helmet; the only time you ever got a word out of him, he said gruffly (but not unpleasantly) that he had nightmares about being crushed by a falling safe. The elderly lady who flutters around the Powell turntable every day, trying to give a transfer to somebody for a free ride. After months she finally consented to explain: "I ride the Market Street car downtown every day and I always ask for a transfer I don't need. I give it away to a person waiting for a cable. It's my little good deed for the day." Then she looked frightened and darted off. One doesn't talk to strangers. . . .

The people all around—close enough to touch, impossible to reach. Old men in little hotel lobbies; you're afraid to look at them for fear they'll think you're pitying them. Old women shopping alone in the late grocery stores; you nod and smile as you both reach for the same apple, but her eyes look through you—to what? A better life, long gone? You'll never know. Twelve people hurtling upward in an elevator, each with his own personal misery—each as far away as an astronaut in a capsule. Hello Out There! But nobody answers. . . .

People, people everywhere, yours and mine and nobody's, a sea of faceless faces— all alike, all different. The fine-looking man in the Homburg who turns out

STRANGERS
IN A
CROWDED
ROOM

to be a janitor on his day off. The waiter who owns a string of apartment houses and is richer than his employer. The newsboy who turns first to the financial section to see how his stocks are doing. The Kearny Street millionaire who walks to work to save fifteen cents. The bartender who'll book you a bet, get you a fix, find you an illegal doctor—and see you in church every Sunday. The strange girls of what's left of the Tenderloin, tripping to breakfast at 2 P.M., their hair in curlers under garish scarves, wearing too much make-up and not enough underwear. All with something in common, all people whose paths crisscross daily, all with nothing to say to each other.

The city rattles and roars, creaks and groans under its load of humanity, racing along parallel lines that never meet, going around in tiny circles that never quite touch. In the Heights, where life is the sum of its parties, they stand nose to nose at the cocktail hour, their thoughts a million miles away, although their glasses meet in midair. In the Sunset, they live cheek-by-jowl, enacting their personal joys and tragedies in solitary refinement. On Skid Road, they walk their lonely miles, trusting nothing but the bottles in their hands, knowing no warmth but the cold liquid. In the office buildings, they smile in the halls and go into their shells— a desk away.

Ah yes, the parties. A particularly fine one is going on in Mr. Melvin Belli's ornately precious law offices on Montgomery Street—an old mahogany bar as central motif, chandeliers glittering over old law books, old cronies, crones young and old. Judges are there, properly sober and hoping to remain so. Mr. Jake Ehrlich is there, exuding immaculate white linen from every pore. Pretty girls and thick slices of turkey and your glass never allowed to become empty.

Outside, two automobiles come together in the sickening sound of the times: grinding metal, splinter and spray of glass, an awful hush broken by a hubcap clattering free down the street, slower and slower and then the brrrrrr-clop as it comes to rest. The lawyers make jokes. A few pull out their business cards and head for the crash, laughing, still clutching their highball glasses. The president of a big insurance firm shoulders them aside. "For once," he guffaws, "I'm gonna get there first."

They see the two smashed cars locked together, like fighting bulls. The driver of one is unconscious. The other, an attractive girl, is in shock, sitting behind the broken steering wheel, her eyes staring sightlessly, her broken right arm angled crazily. From the walls and nooks and crannies, up from the sewers, come the gawkers, some with flash cameras. She gazes unblinking into their exploding bulbs.

An ambulance crew tenderly pries her out of the car. She is wearing a black dress and pearls, and a stole is strewn on the front seat. So she was on her way to dinner, to meet her date. The lawyers stand and watch, still sipping their drinks, as the ambulance pulls away. Through the crowd walks a Chinese boy, a wooden box under his arm, and he is chanting "Shine, shoeshine, who wants a shine," and you wonder who was waiting where for the girl in the black dress and pearls. . . .

Don't call it Frisco. Call it San Francisco, call it beautiful and bright, dirty and ugly, watch the neon elevators rise in the new towers, see the funny lady hit the pigeons with her umbrella, hear the cars crash and the Christmas carols floating out over Post Street in the Year of Our Lord

I suppose it's important and even salubrious to get away from it all now and then, but when "all" is a city like San Francisco, I'm not so sure. Maybe that's because I'm a city boy at heart, and love it, with all its muck and guck, its grifters and graffiti, its misters and misery. We may have evil-smelling busses, but have you sniffed a skunk lately? Is carbon monoxide worse than poison oak? Besides, we have full-time peace pickets on Mission Street, and I haven't heard about any being on duty at Azusa, Cucamonga, or even Colusa.

To appreciate life as a city boy, you have to be composed of equal parts of masochism, sadism, sentimentality, and slobbism. You have to be shifty, crafty, nimble-footed, quick-witted, and suffused with a burning love-hate for all mankind. On the bus, beat the old lady to the seat, but get up for the pretty girl. Waiting in a crowd for a cab, elbow your way to the front of the pack; ten points if you knock over an elderly party on a cane. "Walk" when the signal says "wait." Park in red zones, and if it'll help, paste a "FUNERAL" sticker on your windshield. When nobody's looking, kick a pigeon or an old man feeding one. Leave a four-bit tip for a six-bit drink, but spend thirty seconds deciding whether to put a nickel or a dime in the parking meter. It's a hard life, but filled with rewards. The country boy would never understand.

A city boy might get lost on the Dipsea Trail, but in his own way he is filled with as much recondite information as a Sierra Club guide. On rainy days he knows which buildings to take short cuts through. In a split second he can identify that distant siren as police, fire, or ambulance. He doesn't size up the wind by wetting a finger; he glances at the Telephone Building to see whether the red flag is flying (storm warning) or Old Glory (peace, it's wonderful). Even when the sun is shining on Montgomery, he can hear the first foghorn blasting from the Gate, and he knows the gray wave will soon be rolling over Russian Hill. He never stands in line at a restaurant; he sneaks in through the back door and perches at the bar, whence his favorite waiter will soon lead him to the choice table somebody else has been waiting an hour for. These are sweet triumphs untasted in Medford or Marysville.

People—that's what a city has more of than anything else, and the city boy learns how to mingle with them without being swallowed up by them. He seldom catches their names, but he knows their faces by heart, and only the city has them: the broken-nosed fighter peddling papers, the shoeshine boy who looks like Sammy Davis (and thinks he is), the Powell Street newsie who wears a brown derby and a perennial cigar butt in the corner of his mouth, the couples heading for matinees at the St. Francis (hotel, not theater), the Little Old Lady of Market Street who swears like a longshoreman at anybody who gets in her way, the blind man who says "Hi" before you do, the old pensioners South o' Market who wear their hats indoors and out and gold heirloom chains (grandfather's) across their spotted vests—and seem more typical of the real San Francisco than anybody since Sunny Jim, steam beer, and the ferry with the calliope on her deck.

Scenery? Schmeenery. As far as the city boy is concerned, when you've seen one

redwood, you've seen 'em all. His are the days and nights of the thousand and one sights: the cable car wobbling into the clutch of waiting passengers, pennants fluttering from tall towers whose façades are as familiar as the faces of loved ones, narrow streets wandering up and down the hills as though lost, and a long hook 'n' ladder threading its swivel-hipped way down Market like a broken-field runner while the warning bells pound at the street corners and traffic halts as though somebody had stopped a movie film. There are the endless wonders of the shopwindows—the treasures and the junk—and baby orchids all in a row on a sidewalk flower stand. All this and an army of girls with lovely legs to trail along Post Street, past the doormen, past the off-duty movie ushers with suit jackets over uniform pants, past the chauffeurs dusting limousines and the young men pushing cases of clothing on roller-skate wheels.

A city like San Francisco—there is nothing like it in Pleasanton or Provence. Flotsam, jet set, the Harbor Police and fireboats spraying like a fountain afloat. Nudes, prudes, ready Eddy Street girls, pretty boys whose pants are too tight, FM, AM, Channel 9, and a "Tower of Music" eighty-one stories in the sky. In the far country, all is silence. Here there is the never-ending sound of laughter and despair, the ugly-beautiful sound of people.

San Francisco is a clubby kind of town. Any four men who meet once a week for lunch eventually come to think of themselves as a "club," even if they never do anything more (or less) important than talk about girls and shake dice for the check.

The financial district especially is studded with clubby little groups, organized on the misery-loves-company basis. A lot of them meet daily in the Commercial and Merchants Exchange Clubs, where they can experience the joys of Togetherness while looking thoughtful over a sandwich and dominoes, a game that makes as much noise as children building blocks and is every bit as exciting. All this is good, innocent fun and adds tone to the city. The only clubs not to be countenanced are those that take themselves seriously and sell insignia to be worn on the breast of blue blazers.

Louis Lurie has been running his own club in a corner of Jack's restaurant for thirty-odd years; its only unifying bond is that everybody has to eat what Mr. Lurie eats, and he'll give $100 to anybody who can grab the check before he does (he hasn't lost yet).

John A. Vietor, the publisher of a San Francisco magazine, hosts a "club" that meets regularly at Trader Vic's. This group includes the fairest flower of the local literary establishment: Mark Schorer, Herbert Gold, Niven Busch, Barnaby Conrad, Blair Fuller, Arthur Hoppe, Hugh Chisholm, and Pierre Salinger, who was a newspaperman once himself. The membership is full and there is a long hating list waiting for Mr. Vietor to pick up the whole check.

And so it goes. Vanessi's has the Calamari Club, noted principally for the sly humor of politicians (calamari is the Italian word for squid, I squid you not), and

Kearny Street, near California

The San Franciscans and Their Clubs

Bardelli's is home base for the Retired Bookmakers of Daly City. As for the Saints 'n' Sinners, once a thriving luncheon club, it went the way of all clubs that take themselves seriously. As soon as it began doing charitable deeds, like giving milk to people who prefer martinis, it was doomed.

I don't mean to ignore the formal and Very Important clubs. Nob Hill's Pacific Union, sometimes known as the Second City Hall, still runs the town, for better or worse. The Burlingame Club hangs onto society's reins with a grip (and sometimes head) of iron. The Bohemian Club is noted for its handsome building and its popovers. No artist or writer of exceptional talent has hung around the place since poet George Sterling, who showed his true feelings in the end by killing himself on the premises. Sterling was a great friend of Jack London, the socialist, and wouldn't be allowed in today. The Olympic Club is full of muscular types standing at the bar. When one of them says, "I can lick any guy in the house," you'd better believe it. The University Club has a swell view of the Bay. As for the Family, what is there to say about a club with a name like that? You hope they're kidding, but you know they aren't.

Getting back to the more informal clubs, I was invited to a meeting of one of the newest and most thriving (I get invited to every club—once). Called La Marmite, it meets weekly at the estimable Hotel de France, in North Beach, run by a Basque gentleman named Claude Berhouet.

Marmite is a French word for pot, which all the members have, because all they do each week is drink Pernod and water, eat good food, drink good French wine, lace their coffee with anise and cognac, and talk about how the food in France has gone to hell. Nobody is trying to do anything for anybody except maybe pass the *pommes de terre dorée*. You can't beat a club like that.

The day I was there was a very special one, because Lucien Heyraud was doing the cooking. For long golden years Lucien was the most celebrated chef in San Francisco. When he presided over the kitchens of the Palace Hotel, the food was extravagant and magnificent and the wine cellar filled with rare vintages. Then Mr. Sheraton bought the place and began counting the pats of butter, at which point Lucien went into retirement, not to mention a funque bleu.

For this meeting of La Marmite, Lucien emerged from his Marina house, put on his old white uniform, placed his chef's cap atop his soufflé of a face, and went to work. First he made a Caesar salad with shrimp. "This is my little joke," he said. "It was invented in Los Angeles, where it is considered the highest form of culinary art. It is undoubtedly the lowest."

Then he served a beef Stroganoff. "Now this is a joke too," he said, smiling a wicked smile. "When you run a restaurant you buy strips of filet. There is always a piece not so good at the end. Instead of throwing it away, you slice it thin, disguise it under this strong sauce and give it an exotic name. Beef Stroganoff. Ridiculous. Absolutely unknown in Russia." (Loud cries of "But that is so true!" from Dimitri "Poom" de Ralguine, a true Russian.)

For dessert, a golden custard. "Because I don't feel like working," said Lucien. But under Heyraud's magic touch it was all superb, and let it not be said that the

Châteauneuf-du-Pape '57 and the Taittinger Blanc de Blancs '55 didn't help, because they did. Good food, good wine, and an uncharitable attitude toward peanut butter-and-jelly sandwich lunches should be enough to keep any club together.

A reader writes, or did once, "As a newcomer to San Francisco, I am confused by the constant newspaper references to a district known as Pacific Heights, which I cannot find on any map of the city. Where—and what—is it?"

One is tempted to reply that Pacific Heights is a mythical faubourg that exists only in the minds of society editors and real estate agents, but that wouldn't be entirely accurate. For there really is a Pacific Heights, with its own peculiar view of San Francisco—perhaps the only view in town that looks inward rather than out.

Literally, Pacific Heights is a bit of a misnomer. Since it lies on the northern flank of the city, it overlooks the bay, not the Pacific. Physically, its boundaries are as loose as its restrictions are tight—let us say, from around Fillmore to Presidio, and from Clay to Union (westward from Presidio to about Arguello the section becomes Presidio Heights, with no marked difference in income or outlook).

However, as you may infer from these loose delineations, there is more to Pacific Heights than location, for many poor or socially unacceptable people live in the areas sketched above, and to be Really Pacific Heights you may not be either. But as long as you are neither, you may even live on Russian, Nob, or Telegraph Hills, and, in rare instances, Sea Cliff or even Jordan Park (*very* rare). Potrero Hill may make it yet, but never St. Francis Wood.

A further salient of Pacific Heights juts down the Peninsula into parts of Burlingame, Hillsborough, and Woodside, somehow avoiding Atherton almost completely. The late Mr. Atherton would be astounded.

In sum, Pacific Heights is a point of view that points at itself with pride. Ideally, it is Old Money, which, as anybody knows, is much better than the new, inflated stuff. It is Pucci pants, little Chanel suits, English bootmakers and an accent compounded of the proper upbringing, Ivy League schools, and Old Forester.

Pacific Heights is "Let's hop in the Jag and buzz down to Pebble for the weekend." It's knowing Paris much better than Los Angeles, New York better than Oakland, and the Right People in both. It's "couldn't be nicer, couldn't be more attractive, couldn't be more fun" and couldn't have been duller, with or without the quotes. It's saying on long weekends, "Let's go away—*everybody* will be out of town anyway."

Pacific Heights is houseboys in white jackets walking poodles in clipped jackets, polished windows with shades drawn by polished butlers, indifferent dinners cooked by indifferent cooks ("good ones are *so* hard to get"), surprisingly strong martinis and surprisingly bad wines. The houses are pleasant, whether done in Early Michael Taylor or Late Anthony Hail, and the mirrors are generally superior to, and looked at more often than, the pictures. As the finger bowls come, the ladies go to powder their noses.

Pacific Heights is that eternal cocktail party at which everybody knows everybody else, an endless bridge game involving the identical foursomes, musical chairs to the same old tune, packages from Gump's, I. Magnin, Podesta and Laykin, Tues-

From Presidio and the beginning of Golden Gate Bridge
across Pacific Heights and Russian Hill to downtown and the Bay Bridge

day and Friday nights at the opera and a third-base box at Candlestick. If you're not With It, where are you?

Through all the changes it changes not. It is the city's power and sometimes glory, the Northern Lights and the Southern Cross, the day-and-night repository of all that is gilded and glamorous about San Francisco. It is big business and big pleasure, and it keeps a lot of money in circulation, occasionally its own. And if it sometimes appears to be out of touch with reality, weep not. Reality could very well be out of touch with Pacific Heights.

Without Pacific Heights—and let me stress again that I use the term loosely—San Francisco would not be what it is today. To the world of stylish travelers and slick magazine editors, it *is* San Francisco—or at least the part of it that is thought of (and written about) as "sophisticated, gay, and sparkling." When any distinguished visitor says, "I just adore San Francisco," you may be sure he isn't referring to picnics in Golden Gate Park or the English muffins at Foster's. He has been taken in by The Group, he has been given the Pacific Heights whirl, and this, forevermore, is San Francisco to him.

He is one of the fortunate few, for The Group is as clannish as its counterparts anywhere (visitors who say San Francisco is "cold" and "hard to get to know" didn't make it through the gates). The cable cars, the bridges and Twin Peaks are fine to see, but if you haven't been invited into the hushed drawing rooms, where the minions of Thomas the Butler pass the canapés, you haven't been inside the San Francisco where names are dropped and unlisted phone numbers picked up.

So I say hail to Pacific Heights, wherever it may be. As the city grows away from itself, it grows more deeply into itself, perhaps in self-protection. It is the last of the constants, where children still curtsy, manners are excellent, the ladies are lovely, and drinking a bit too much is not only acceptable but almost mandatory. Life may be equally pleasant in the Deep Mission or the Far Sunset, but Pacific Heights has the panache and the postiche, not to mention the Beluga and the Malassol, and the Aubusson underfoot.

Whatever high style still accrues to San Francisco lives on in this glorious Never-Never Land of three cars for every two-car garage and chicken à la Kiev in every pot. Long may it be preserved, sous cloche or on the rocks.

As some of the great old houses disappear, an authentic slice of Old San Francisco—the "Chinaman's Room"—is disappearing, too. The new boxlike cubicles, many of them innocent of basements, make no provision for this onetime necessity, and that's about the only nice thing I can think to say about them.

San Francisco's Chinese rightly resent the westerners' use of the word "Chinaman," with its overtones of condescension and undertones of derision, and I hope they'll understand that I'm using it here only for historical reasons.

In order to have a "Chinaman's Room"—and practically all the vintage houses have them—you need a basement and a Chinese servant, fresh from the Orient, lost in the New World, willing to work seven days a week and live in a rough-boarded box with a chicken-wire door, back in the darkest corner behind the furnace.

Those days are over—but when they were at their height, generations ago, a sort of paternalistic serfdom flourished in Rich San Francisco. Every family of means had its Chinaman, an inscrutable white-jacketed man who became "like one of the family," in the hollow phrase of the Old South, and adopted the family name, his own being pointless in the anonymity of his life. Old San Francisco was full of Sing Won Murphys and Shew Poy Joneses and Kee Smiths, and even, I suppose, a Hop Long Cassidy.

Along the gilt-edge streets overlooking the Pacific, you still see a few of the wrinkled old retainers around, burning leaves in the gutter, polishing the brasswork, or simply sitting at a window and staring out to sea, presumably dreaming of the good old days when a Chinese could at least go back to the homeland in a wooden box to sleep with his ancestors. That was before the Bamboo Curtain, of course.

One prominent family I know has a Chinese cook who has been handed down from generation to generation, like an heirloom. They call him "Casey." It's an old family joke. In deference to his age, he has been promoted upstairs from the "Chinaman's Room" to a space off the laundry room, near the back porch. He putters around in tennis shoes and mutters over the stove in absolutely indecipherable pidgin English.

Much to my surprise, I saw him one summer Sunday in a gambling joint on the south side of Tahoe, a passable blonde at his side. He was playing roulette, and when he saw me, he winked. "Don't tell missy," he said. "She think I spend my day off in the temple, praying for my ancestors." There was hardly a trace of pidgin in his English.

The next time I had dinner with "Casey's family"—well, that's the way they like to think of themselves, when they're being warm and lovable—there was Casey, shuffling around as usual in his tennis shoes, his open white jacket flopping over his baggy pants, a skullcap on the back of his head.

"How are you, Casey? I said as he came slithering out of the kitchen, slightly bent, his hands crossed and up his sleeves—playing the Heathen Chinee bit to the hilt.

"Okay, mistah," he said. "But work too hard. Missy velly tough cookie. Wish I back in Chlina wit' forefaddas."

"What a character," laughed his mistress. "We love him. He's like a child."

Casey paused on his way back to the kitchen and gave me a wink over the top of her head. "Okay," he cackled. "Now I go make dinnah chop-chop." A character, all right.

Some years ago Dr. Samuel R. Sherman bought a handsome old house in the 2800 block of Pacific Avenue—a vast red brick pile with more rooms than the busy doctor at first had time to explore. After he'd been in about two weeks, he got a phone call from the previous owner.

"Sorry to bother you, Doctor," he said, "but we've had a wonderful old Chinaman in the family for years—he loved us and our house. Practically grew up in it. I wonder if you could find something for him to do around the house—gardening, housework, anything."

Grant Avenue. St. Mary's Church, and Chinatown, center

"Certainly," answered Dr. Sherman. "How do I get in touch with him?"

There was a silence, and then the other replied, "Well, I don't know. I imagine he's still in the basement."

Grabbing a flashlight, the doctor prowled far down into the bowels of the mansion. In a corner he spied a door he'd never noticed before. Inside "the China-man's Room" he found the old man. He'd been sitting there patiently ever since the old master had moved out, waiting for instructions from the new.

I was looking at a house on Scott Street one time, and as we were inspecting the cellar we came to an airless room with a rough wooden floor and one tiny window high up. It bore the musty smell of the ages. "This is the Chinaman's Room," the real estate man said briskly, "but if you don't have a Chinaman, it'd be perfect for your dog." The dog, a poodle with all the refinement and sensibilities of the French, poked her nose inside, recoiled, bounded up the stairs, and never, to my knowledge, went near the cellar again.

Our city has a neon ghetto and it is Grant Avenue in Chinatown. An old woman is crossing the street, wearing black pantaloons, a long smock—and white tennis shoes. The guy with you says, grinning: "A member of the Wong Birch Society?" You smile too, the fatuous, chauvinistic smirk of the Caucasian in Chinatown.

Ah, we do make such sport of the Chinese; it's almost like the good old "Yellow Peril" days of Dennis Kearney and William Randolph Hearst the Elder. Two Wongs don't make a white. The phone book is full of Wong numbers. The Tai Ping Company—do they teach the touch system? Mr. Pon Gee, the insurance man—no doubt with a silky manner. Some chop suey and flied lice, Cholly, and make it chop-chop. As Charlie well knows, you don't have to go overseas to find the Ugly American. We may all locate him in the mirror.

Still, I suppose, you could say the little old lady has come a long way. Fifty years ago, she would have been tottering painfully along Dupont Gai on bound feet. The menfolk were wearing long robes and pigtails, heading toward the smell of opium in the Street of the Thousand Lanterns. Arnold Genthe, the noted photographer, was lurking in dark corners, snapping the pictures that would engrave forever the image of Chinatown that lives today only in the minds of Caucasians.

Don't get me wrong: San Franciscans love Chinatown, as well they should. It's one of our most consistent tourist attractions—"the largest Chinese settlement outside the Orient" (a polite way of saying ghetto). Everybody has his favorite little side-street restaurant, "and we know it's good because you only see Chinese there" (this is more likely to mean it's cheap than good). For ads and photographs, it's hard to beat: the silhouette of a pagoda rooftop, a dragon-entwined street lamp with a halo of fog, a jumble of neon ideographs, vaguely sinister-looking men, eyes hidden beneath black hat brims.

To those who don't live in it, Chinatown is San Francisco's most frozen cliché. Clink of mah-jongg tiles behind drawn curtains in a back alley. Dried sea horses in an herbalist's window, winter melon and snow peas at the grocer's, meat-filled buns in the bakery. Memories of tong wars and "Little Pete."

That's Chinatown—that and the great dragon snaking through the mobs on New Year's. That and the fortune cookies and the chopsticks and the Midwestern tourists who buy back-scratchers and complain that they "can't find anything from China in Chinatown." They don't realize that we don't do business with China because there is no China; all the Chinese come from Taiwan.

If you live in Chinatown, you live in a slum. Behind the neon and the bars and the restaurants and the curio shops, that's what it is—one big tenement, dirty, overcrowded and diseased (the TB rate is the highest in town). Have you ever walked up those long, narrow stairs, past all the mailboxes that the tourists find so colorful? I have. You climb into a musty past of tiny wooden cubicles.

But the message never seems to get through the impermeable wall of fortune cookies and guidebooks. At regular intervals, a group of Chinatown leaders complain at City Hall about the slum conditions, the need for a master plan, the fact that 90 per cent of the buildings qualify for condemnation and should be replaced by redevelopment.

Early look at Chinatown at Washington and Grant

108

Sam Wah restaurant

Downtown oasis bounded by Geary, Powell, Post and Stockton Streets

Redevelop a tourist attraction? Heaven forbid. Even so intelligent a man as Planning Director James R. McCarthy was as taken aback as a member of the Convention & Visitors Bureau. He said things like "We mustn't destroy the character of Chinatown—one of the city's prime tourist attractions." The narrow streets and old buildings "are important to the image of San Francisco as an urban and urbane place to live."

Especially if you don't live there. The Chinese aren't people, they're characters in a four-color billboard. The Chinese bankers, lawyers, and architects who complain about the restrictions on Chinatown aren't typical; to the planners and the Convention Bureau and most of the rest of us, the Chinese do your laundry, cook, wait on tables, and show you how to use chopsticks.

When they aren't on tap, being smiling and servile to their betters, they disappear up those long stairs into their rabbit warrens—non-people living in a tacky Disneyland.

I can hear it now: "Everybody likes the Chinese in San Francisco." Sure they (we) do, in a paternalistic way. "Besides, they like to stick together" (or are they stuck together?). The young, the quick, and the smart are getting out of Chinatown, or as far out as they're allowed. They aren't taken in by the role they're supposed to play, nor will they, and they aren't fooled by the phony pagoda rooftops that look so picturesque on the skyline but merely cover a multitude of sins. That little old lady in tennis shoes is still one step behind. Her daughter is wearing high heels and looking for a way out of "dreamy, dreamy Chinatown."

Sometimes you look around and wonder: Is it all going to pot? The hands on the Ferry Building clock stand at five minutes to midnight and the lights on Coit Tower grow dimmer. . . .

If you love San Francisco, that's the way it seems at times—but there's a way to shake that feeling. You walk the streets and ride the busses and wander through the alleys of North Beach, where, even in the rain, it always seems like spring in Livorno. And you look at the people, the crazy people of San Francisco—the stuffed shirts and the nuts, the happy drunks and the drunk with power, the senior citizens in Union Square, waving their arms in endless argument under gray clouds of pigeons and the monument to victory in Manila Bay so many thousands of years ago.

A Mission Street bus. There's not much glamor about a bus. It doesn't have the rocketing, racketing verve of an old iron monster of a streetcar. But this one, snorting along in the truculent way of busses, has a couple of characters aboard—high at high noon.

On the front bench, a guy with one leg and crutches. "Hey, bartender," he keeps calling to the driver, "how about a beer?" No reply. Faint smiles from the women. The guy pounds his crutches on the deck. "I'm drunk," he announces beatifically. "Me-me-me. Drunk Do-re-me-fa-me-me-me drunk and gonna get drunker."

A man in the back who looks like a longshoreman—open shirt, white cap—shakes his head. "Poor guy, poor, one-legged drunk." He's drunk himself. "Gotta get off and get myself a drink." He stands on the back treadle, eyeing a nervous young man in a narrow Ivy League uniform seated alongside.

"Hiya, buddy, "says the longshoreman. Ivy uniform manages a pale smile. The longshoreman lays a horny paw on his arm. "How about me buying you a drink at the next stop?" Now all eyes are on them, and Ivy League's eyes roll around in mild panic. "Thanks, old man," he says with false heartiness. "I'm-uh-on my way to the Palace to meet a friend for lunch."

"Sounds great, just great," says the longshoreman. "Mind if I join you?" Ivy uniform turns red. "You don't like the way I'm dressed," sighs the longshoreman patiently. "Tellya what, I'll get all dressed up tonight and we'll have dinner. When I'm dressed up I look like an angel. Beautiful."

The bus stops, the rear door opens. "How about it, buddy?" says the long-shoreman, standing there on the step. Ivy becomes desperate. "You'll miss your stop," he says, pushing the longshoreman roughly out the door. The bus rolls on and the other passengers look at the narrow Ivy League uniform reprovingly. His manners assert themselves. "I'm sorry," he says in a taut voice. "I-uh-I'm sorry." He leaves at the next stop, hurriedly, looking down.

You get off at Third and walk toward Market to a pawnshop where a man is trying out an accordion. "O Sole Mio," played badly, sounds weird on Third Street. On Market, along comes a fine, strange figure of a man—bearded and erect, swinging a cane, a muffler arranged neatly around his neck, his cowboy boots polished. The passers-by look at him and laugh. Until they see the big button on his lapel. "I Am Blind."

In a cafeteria, you sit down next to Bill Branch, who's eating alone. Along comes an old-timer in a cowboy shirt, who plops himself down and starts talking, just like that: "They don't build bridges like they useta. It's this younger generation of upstart engineers—all outsiders from back East." After glancing around, he whispers, "The Bay Bridge is going to collapse and I will tell you why. It's the paint! You know how much paint they put on that bridge every year? Twenty-five *tons*."

He is deadly serious. "Now then," he says, pounding the table, "Multiply twenty-five tons a year by twenty-five years and you get six hundred and twenty-five *tons* of paint a-l-l p-r-e-s-s-i-n-g D-O-W-N on that bridge!" He ends on a note of triumph.

"There's only one thing to do," he trumpets, wagging a finger. "Scrape if off! Before somebody gets killed!"

You walk around and ride around, and what do you see? At Powell and Market, a kid, about eight, with a string lasso and a paper bag, catching pigeons. While you watch, he nails three. The cop nearby looks the other way, elaborately. In front of the Golden Rule Café, another drunk—this one a big, burly blond guy who falls down twice, heavily. A cop tries to pick him up. "Gimme one more chance, coach," he mumbles. "I know I can make that first down." The cop smiles and the customers cheer.

Forgive the newspaperman if he is often moody, sometimes neurotic, almost always frustrated. For the news of a city is hard to come by, difficult to put into words. Some of the best stories are never written, although most of the worst are. He is tormented by the certain knowledge that he is reporting only the obvious, seldom getting to the heart and roots of a city's day-to-day existence.

His tools are still too primitive—the hit-and-miss of personal contact. In the age-old tradition of his craft, he can do no better than pick up the phone or walk down the street, asking plaintively: "What's new?"

"What's new?" shrugs the cop on the Kearny Street beat, staring into space. "Nothing is new, that's what's new. What else is new is that I've never seen it so quiet." But even as he smiles and nods, the reporter knows he's wrong, for the city is never quiet. In the old streets of the Mission, on the wooded slopes of Mount Sutro, in the new world of the Golden Gateway, under the fog-shrouded trees of Golden Gate Park, the news is constantly breaking, like the waves around Land's End. But sometimes it breaks unseen, unheard . . .

"Town's dead," grumps the cabbie, slumping down behind his wheel and taking a fresh bite on his cigar. He's wrong too. It's just that the news is sometimes subtle. The sport-jacketed man walking past: a night club owner, heavily in debt, on his way for a final deal that will save his monogrammed shirt, his initialed Cadillac, his engraved gold lighter. The attractive blond girl staring into the nearby show window: she has just been to her lawyer, to sign a complaint against the married man who fathered her new baby girl (the columns will identify him merely as "L."). The tense little man who hops into the grumpy cabbie's cab and orders, "Airport, please": an auditor who has been juggling his company's books, and is flying to Las Vegas for a last chance to get even (the column items will be vague, until the grand jury indictment comes through).

Anything stirring? "Look for yourself," sighs the bartender, waving his bar cloth around the dark saloon. The reporter looks at the handful of customers—not a printable item in the lot. The gray-haired, expensively dressed woman alone at the bar, who orders her drinks in Tenderloin jargon: "Straight shot, water back"—the widow of a man who was beloved on Montgomery Street; if she's lucky and waits long enough, the bartender will go home with her. The two guys lost in a drone of conversation in the corner: one has a phony proposition that'll make a fast buck "for everybody," the other knows The Right Wrong Guy to see at City Hall. The sullen cocktail waitress: her senile millionaire isn't keeping her any longer, and it's hell to have to work again. All the news that's fit, we print. The rest is libel.

Nothing new: The reporter walks slowly down the street, jingling the small change in his pocket. The newsboy at Geary and Powell shouts a headline that broke three thousand miles away. A hood who is wanted in a dozen cities leans against a lamppost, his hard face shadowed under a dark hat, and chats with a bookie whose big nose inspired the nickname everybody knows—even the cops. In the dim distance, a siren wails. The guys on the police beat will cover it. Probably nothing. Penny-ante fire. A shooting with no class . . .

"You're nice to come," greets the host in his Russian Hill flat, smiling his white-toothed smile. He is wearing a velvet jacket, and he proves (again) how fluent he is in four languages as he moves around the drawing room, introducing his other guests. "You won't get any news here," he says, grinning, showing his dimples (again), "we're all MUCH too respectable." You join the group admiring the view. The fading Peninsula beauty in the dazzling emeralds, who's carrying on an outrageous affair with the young man in the silk dinner suit; everybody knows about it, including her fat husband, but nobody talks about it, for this is polite society. The tired looking blonde, married to a title with a mansion here, a castle in Ireland, a villa in Italy: she has everything, and goes daily to an analyst to find out why she's miserable. The old bachelor who can be counted on to fill out a dinner party because "he's SUCH fun"; some of the stranger spots in North Beach think he's fun too, till he falls down drunk. But the host was right. No news here.

"Naaah, nothin'," drawls the newsman to his city editor, hunching the phone between his ear and shoulder. "Let's wrap it up and go home. The town is closed, man, locked tight." But even as he yanks the empty copy paper out of his typewriter with a sudden viciousness, he knows he's wrong—for the stories are breaking minute by minute in the dark and jumbled city. Behind the drawn curtains of a Nob Hill love nest at 2 A.M. In the skyscrapers of the financial district, where a few lights are always burning and the wastebaskets are bulging with news that will be lost forever in the incinerator. In a Chinatown alley, where the men file up the narrow stairs at 4 A.M., the last man pausing for a second to make sure they aren't being followed. At a certain address on a certain side street in North Beach, where the acrid smell of marijuana is always in the air. If the noise that nobody hears isn't really noise, the news that nobody can print isn't really news. The reporter bangs his typewriter carriage in disgust, claps on his hat, and goes out for a nightcap in the "club" that opens at 2 A.M. and runs till dawn.

"Dull night," remarks the cop behind the wheel of the squad car as he heads back to the Hall of Justice. "Suits me," says his partner. "I'm ready for the sack." But the city never really sleeps, and the 1001 tales of Baghdad-by-the-Bay are being enacted everywhere, anywhere, always.

"What's new?" you ask William Saroyan in a Russian Hill apartment. A log is blazing in the fireplace (where else are the fireplaces working in August?). Outside the picture window (where else do windows open on such pictures?) a Dutch freighter painted a startling blue is heading for the Orient. A tug is chasing an incoming tanker, like a toddler trying to catch up with Papa. A sunset burns through the fog hiding the Gate Bridge, and Tamalpais stands out with the thin sharpness of a Japanese print.

"What's new," says Saroyan, squinting at the view through a martini dryly, "is that I drove out here from New York in an old Lincoln limousine—a real gangster model. Doing a piece about it for the *Saturday Evening Post*. Saw a lot of things I've always wanted to see—Gutzon Borglum's heads of the presidents on Mount Rushmore: Washington, Jefferson, Teddy Roosevelt and—who's the fourth? That's

right—Lincoln, the only one we should remember. Finally saw Old Faithful in Yellowstone. A disappointment. It erupts every thirty or ninety minutes, depending on its mood. When it made up its mind to go, it was just a tiny brrrrp. Maybe it was embarrassed—so many people watching."

It always seems like San Francisco when Bill Saroyan is around. With his booming voice and his eternal exuberance, he makes you feel younger. He's pushing sixty now, and his bristling mustache is streaked with gray, but his eyes are still amazed and delighted; he is forever Aram.

When you see Saroyan, you remember the struggling young writer in his room on Carl Street, getting one rejection slip after another (and returning them to the editors with a scrawled "I reject your rejection"). You remember him hitting tennis balls over the fence in the park (shouting in wonder, "Look at that ball *go!*") and starving all day in the Main Library, reading anything and everything, filling his empty stomach with great gulps of water from the nearby fountain.

San Francisco was Saroyan in an eleven-dollar overcoat heading for the bookie joint in Opera Alley, playing stud in a North Beach backroom, gambling with pennies and nickels in the old Menlo Club—and always writing, writing, in great outgoing bursts. Then came success, and the daring young man was a literary lion. Anita Zabala Howard gave a party for him in her Nob Hill penthouse, and he was the last to arrive ("My streetcar was late and I had to transfer"). When his Pulitzer Prize-winning play, "The Time of Your Life," opened at the Curran, we were able to shout, "Author! Author!" for the first time in *our* young lives.

Star Eddie Dowling peered over the footlights after the curtain had dropped, but the author was nowhere to be seen. As necks craned, Dowling got off a magnificent ad lib: "Now, surely he can't be out picking grapes at THIS hour." He was in the bar next door, buying drinks.

When he is back, the city regains some of its old rollicking vitality. He asked for another martini and gazed out at the sunset. "Sure, the city has changed," he said, "But that's good, isn't it? Everything has to change. I used to gamble to lose, now I try to win. I even appear on shows like *Candid Camera* and take it with great seriousness. You'd be surprised how serious I can get now about five thousand dollars." He had with him a copy of his book—*Not Dying*, the autobiography of a fifty-five-year-old writer. The title is pure Saroyan: "And now, Mr. S.," said the interviewer, "to what do you attribute your old age?"

"Not dying."

The eager tourist, on his first visit to San Francisco, stepped into a cab outside the Hotel St. Francis. Settling into the back seat, he said: "Driver, what do you do for laughs in this town?" In the telegraphic manner of his counterparts everwhere, the cabbie shrugged. "We laugh."

A bit rude, but perfectly true. There has always been laughter on the hills— cackle of crone, shriek of the slightly mad, appreciative chuckle of understatement, delicate tinkle of drawing-room belle, roar of the hearty. Even during the city's mortal agony—the fire and earthquake of 1906—a rollicking humor survived. As the flames were still crackling, signs appeared reading "Eat, Drink and Be Merry, For Tomorrow We Go to Oakland!" And shortly after, when undamaged Fillmore Street began proclaiming itself "The NEW Main Street," the businessmen of Market, already rebuilding their great stores and offices, found time to taunt back:

"Market Street was Market Street when Fillmore was a pup—Market will be Market Street when Fillmore's busted up." Like most valid humor, reasonably prophetic, for Fillmore soon lost its temporary luster.

The earthquake also inspired a classic bit of doggerel by Charles K. Fields, an inveterate rhymster of the day. When it became apparent that Hotaling's big whiskey warehouse had survived the devastation around it, he wrote:

> If, as they say, God spanked the town
> For being over-frisky,
> Why did he burn the churches down
> And spare Hotaling's whiskey?"

Sixty years later, almost to the day, one of the fiercest fires in San Francisco's history destroyed a million dollars' worth of whiskey stored in the San Francisco Warehouse Company, and again a poet was moved to set pen to paper. While the headlines were still fresh, John Klempner wrote this up-to-date version of Fields's classic quatrain:

> Some people say that God is dead—
> A notion I can't purchase;
> For Who burned all that whiskey up
> And spared the city's churches?

A few months after the '06 firequake, the city was shaken by a second major tremor—the graft trials that ended with the conviction of a shrewd little lawyer named Abe Ruef, the hidden power behind the very City Hall that had collapsed, symbolically as well as physically, during the earthquake. After he had been sentenced to fourteen years in San Quentin, for bribery, Ruef was asked by an unfriendly reporter: "Well, Ruef, how does it feel to trade those fancy clothes for a set of stripes?" Here Abe Ruef showed a touch of style. "The zebra," he replied softly, "is not an unbeautiful animal."

A man who would have fitted impeccably into that era, if not its peculations, died in 1966, leaving an unfillable gap. He was Lucius Beebe, the dignified and moneyed dandy who was born in the effete East but was drawn inexorably to what he liked to call "The American West," which he saw as the last best hope of civilized, individualistic man. A prodigious writer in the florid style of his favorite, mauve-tinted epoch, he spent his last—and, by his own admission, happiest—years writing a column for The San Francisco *Chronicle*, filled with extravagant invective against anything more modern than the '37 Rolls-Royce or the '47 French vintages.

(Incidental humorous aside: a columnist for the San Quentin Penitentiary newspaper once observed that the *Chronicle* "has more columns than a Greek temple." Beebe's was definitely Corinthian.)

Beebe moved first to Virginia City in Nevada, a state he admired above all others because it has no income tax. Soon after he had installed himself and his partner, writer-photographer Charles Clegg, in an elegantly refurbished mansion, he was greeted by the then Governor of Nevada, Charles Russell:

"Welcome to Nevada, and thank you for gracing our poor state with your distinguished personages. But I am curious. How can you stand this simple little town after the sophisticated whirl of Manhattan?"

"After all," replied Lucius, twirling his tulip glass, "isn't the life of a peasant in a small town the ultimate sophistication?"

At this, Russell took a sip of his martini and observed that Beebe and Clegg were living in a ten-room house, drinking champagne for breakfast, were being waited on by a formally attired butler, and had the only swimming pool and Rolls-Royces (two) in the county.

"The only peasant I can recall who led an equally simple and austere life," mused the governor, "was Marie Antoinette."

Along with the Virginia City property and the estate he and Clegg later purchased in Hillsborough, Beebe's proudest possession was his private railroad coach, named, of course, "Virginia City." The last time I lunched aboard her—I suppose railway carriages are feminine—she was on a siding in Oakland, making that city look shabbier than usual. A decorator named Robert Hanley had just had her repainted a wild yellow and red on the outside and had refurbished her insides in garish turn-of-the-century décor.

To a crass journalistic question about the cost of the redecorating, Hanley replied, "More than $100,000"—a price Beebe refused to confirm or deny. "The entire subject," he sniffed, "is vulgar in the extreme."

Lunch, prepared by Wallace, the chef, and served by Clarence, the steward, consisted of a Creole fish soup with rice, Southern fried chicken, ham and beans, hot corn bread, pumpkin pie, and a fine dry Bollinger champagne. "Wallace always makes a light lunch," said Beebe. "You should stay for dinner. He's cooking a cow."

Parked next to the "Virginia City" was the private coach of John P. Kiley, then President of the Chicago, Milwaukee & St. Paul Railway. "Frankly, Mr. Kiley's car isn't much inside," said Beebe. "Mrs. Kiley dropped in for a look at ours, and was positively bug-eyed. Turned a sickly green. I don't think Mr. Kiley will ever hear the end of it."

A member of Kiley's staff went through the "Virginia City" a few minutes later and observed, in a small, thin voice: "Very nice." He peered into the service area, looked at the ice container and crowed: "WE have a deep freeze!" "WE," retorted Beebe, "have a Turkish bath." "Oh," said the Kiley man, leaving.

Beebe's favorite luncheon spot in San Francisco was the Garden Court of the Sheraton-Palace Hotel, a vast, glass-domed marble hall with huge crystal chandeliers, great pillars, and ghostly presences. Here, he would often lunch in stately solitude, sipping wine and musing on vanished glories ("His love of the past," columnist Charles McCabe once said, "amounts almost to necrophilia").

I found him one day in the Garden Court, looking particularly morose. "I was just reflecting," he said, "on the tragic fact that there are no more bottles of 1926 Bollinger champagne available anywhere in the world." "What happened to them?" I asked. "I drank them all," he replied lugubriously. On another occasion, a New Year's Eve, he was again alone in the Garden Court, but looking quite content. "At first I was depressed," he confided, "but I finally hit upon a reason to celebrate. As of midnight, all the great wines are one year older!"

In spite of, or perhaps because of, his being an anachronism, Lucius Beebe was a charming, courteous man, with a sense of humor as large as his heart, or even his miraculous liver. I told him one of his favorite stories about himself—an incident that happened at British Motor Cars in San Francisco, after he had picked up one of his Rolls-Royces, in for repairs. After he had driven out, heading for Hillsborough, a mechanic sighed to me: "I hope he makes it okay. How can he see the road with his nose up in the air like that?"

Although we were poles apart politically—politics was a subject we studiously avoided—Beebe and I got along well, and I was deeply touched one day, not too long before his death, when he entrusted me with what he called his "official last words." It is an unusual piece of self-appraisal, and herewith excerpts:

"I find a considerable confusion among the reporters and paragraphers of the land as to just how to describe Beebe, what makes him tick and how to pigeon-hole him, a professional necessity evoked, I imagine, by the brevity of headline space and the necessity of capsule tagging.

"I find myself variously pictured as newspaper publisher, gourmet, clothes-horse, historian of the Old West, owner of a private car and big dog, an alcoholic, no-gooder, wit, poseur phony, no-gooder, a guy who can speak Latin or at least read it, saloon fighter, lammister from New York and no-gooder.

"In a measure all of these are true, but the clothes are too frivolous to mention and the gourmet angle was largely evoked because I once did a Broadway column that included restaurants.

"I admire most of all The Renaissance Man, and, if it can be said without pretentiousness, I like to think of myself as one, at least in small measure. Not a Michelangelo, mark you, but perhaps a poor man's Cellini or road company Cosimo de' Medici. The Medieval Man and Renaissance Man did a number of things, many of them well, a few beautifully. He was no damned specialist.

"I like to think that Chuck [Clegg] and I do a number of things that have no special relationship to one another, some of them passing well. In 'The Territorial Enterprise,' we ran a paper of outrage that was the best of its kind. Our books on the West and railroading are the best we could devise, always beautifully produced and sometimes intelligent. We admire to give good parties and the measure of their success is the number of empties, the size of the restaurant bill and the number of screams for bail during the night.

"If anything is worth doing, it's worth doing in style. And on your own terms and nobody's goddamned else's. I like nice clothes because they are an item in an over-all façade. In themselves they are silly and foppish. I like big houses and hotel suites and a big dog because they become me. Not for ostentation, but because they give me personal pleasure and satisfaction.

"I prefer Rolls-Royces and Bentleys simply and without any equivocation because they are the best. Not just runners-up or compromises, but the best—like Bollinger, Colt's firearms, suits by Henry Pool and traveling Cunard. I kept a private railroad car because it has style and comfort and I am maybe railroad touched in the haid, and anyway, the dog likes it. Also there is no bartender to say, 'That will be all for you, sir.'

"I like people who never give a passing thought to public opinion or the suffrage of society, not who deliberately antagonize it, but simply are unaware that it exists. I like Gene Fowler's aphorism, 'Money is something to be thrown off the back of trains.' If I cease to have the money or the trains, either, I've got memories and may even get good obits if the competition isn't too keen that day.

"I'd like the obits to say: 'Everything he did was made to measure. He never got an idea off the rack.'"

My favorite story about Lucius Beebe synthesizes everything I liked about the man—his undoubted *joie de vivre*, his irreverence, his love of luxury, his wry humor. It happened at a time when Wolcott Gibbs was engaged in writing a profile of Beebe for the *New Yorker* magazine—and they had made an appointment to meet for an interview aboard Beebe's private railway car, parked on a siding at the Pennsylvania Station.

It was a drizzly morning, and Gibbs, clutching his raincoat, was feeling particularly tacky as he made his way gingerly across the intervening tracks. As he approached the private car, Beebe suddenly appeared on the back platform, pink of jowl and clad immaculately in cutaway coat, dove-gray double-breasted vest, striped pants, and spats. Raising aloft a glass of champagne, he called out to the stumbling Gibbs:

"Welcome to Walden Pond!"

The special style of wit that was Lucius Beebe's is gone, but there is always something to smile fondly about in San Francisco. The cable cars, as anachronistic as Beebe himself, are always good for the same kind of chuckle they themselves emit. There was the tourist lady, on her very first visit, who looked at them with great disappointment. "Is THAT all?" she said. "I thought they'd be SUSPENDED from cables." To the tourist who asks: "Do you go to the Top o' the Mark?" there is always the gripman who replies: "Sorry, I can't get in, ma'am—no necktie." And there was the windy day when a Little Old Lady's hat blew off and cartwheeled down the street. She looked questioningly at the gripman, who pouted a small boy pout and folded his hands atop his lever.

"I'm not going to chase it," he announced with great finality. "I'm sick-sick-SICK of being quaint and colorful!"

I was standing on the back platform of a Powell cable one afternoon, next to a small tourist boy who watched with wonderment as the conductor cranked the hand brake. "What's that for?" the boy finally asked. "Well, I'll tell you," replied the conductor pleasantly. "You see that slot down there?" The boy nodded, eyes large. "Now don't tell anybody," the conductor continued, "but an old Chinese gentleman lives down there, and he's so old he can't get up and down this hill without us. There's a very special dingbat at the end of this crank, and we hook onto his pigtail to help him along."

The boy's eyes were positively bursting as the car crossed the top of Nob Hill and started down the other side. "Think we got him okay," said the conductor confidentially, peering into the slot. Then he released the hand brake, looked again, and smote his forehead. "Darn!" he exclaimed. "Lost him!" The tourist boy looked woefully into the slot, almost in tears. "Don't worry, kid," said the conductor jovially. "The next car will get him for sure. It's just that our dingbat needs fixing."

The humor of a city—sometimes as tough, sharp, and bittersweet as city life itself. The Mason Street strippers with the ridiculously contrived names, like the red-haired girl who called herself Strip O'Mycin. One night she said she was tired of that, so I suggested Penny Cillin. "Now certainly," she said witheringly, "a man of your intellectual attainments can think of a better pseudonym." The following night she appeared as Sue de Nimm. The night spots with the equally contrived names—like hungry i and Purple Onion. The hungry i, now owned by Enrico Banducci, was named by its original owner, Eric Nord. The rival Purple Onion was named by—Enrico Banducci. Nearby Finocchio's, which features female impersonators, is known among the In Group as The Italian-Swish Colony. The Manx Hotel on Powell, now eminently respectable, was to the cognoscenti of years gone by, as "the cat house without a tail." The standard joke about San Francisco's imposing Stock Exchange is that the great mural inside was painted by Diego Rivera, a Communist. As for the great statues outside, sculpted by Ralph Stackpole, they have obviously lost their shirts.

If it isn't one thing, it's another to provide amusement in the big city. The now world-famous graffito found on the walls of men's rooms from here to Hamburg—"My mother made me a homosexual," under which is written, "If I send her the yarn, will she make me one?"—originated in the North Beach place known as the Old Spaghetti Factory & Excelsior Coffee House. It was composed by an entertainer named Charles Pierce, whose name is as worthy of recognition as that of the undoubted genius who coined the word "Beatnik" (I bow modestly in my own direction).

And then, each summer, I'm amused all over again by the hopeful banner that flies from the front of a small delicatessen on Geary Boulevard, deep in the city's fog belt. As the horns blow in the near distance, there is that ridiculously cheery message flapping away, almost invisible in the mist. "Let's Have a Picnic," it reads. "Somewhere the Sun Is Shining!"

And so it is, everywhere in any city that still knows how to laugh.

The day started off winsomely enough, with the radio announcer delivering the typical San Francisco weather report: "High fog in the morning, dissipating in the afternoon." Such a pleasant thought, but who wants a hangover at 6 P.M.? I rolled a piece of copy paper into the typewriter and stared out the window at the unlikely city. Purple and magenta freighters were heading out for faraway, glamorous ports, like Coos Bay and San Pedro. A cable car slid down the Hyde Street hill, lost in the grip of a hundred tourists. Deserted Alcatraz dozed in the cool sun—a rock without a role.

"I don't hear that typewriter singing," my wife called out gaily from the next room. Drat. What a wife never understands, as Thurber once said (or was it E. B. White?), is that a writer is working when he looks out the window. I was trying to remember somebody's line about Kearny Street, delivered in the 1880s, when Kearny (pronounced "Carney" then) was the most rollicking thoroughfare in town. "In the space of one block on Kearny," he said, "I could raise a gang to hijack a schooner, topple a statue, rob a bank or set off for a treasure hunt in the Galápagos."

Must have been a swinging street. Still is, in parts. I put the cover back on The Singing Typewriter, stifling it in mid-E, and set out, flat of arch but light of heart, toward Kearny.

Along Chestnut on Russian Hill, burly chauffeurs were walking tiny poodles (the worst part of the job). Pretty nurses were walking rich old ladies. Apartment house doormen were reading racing forms. Sometimes the city looks like a caricature of itself.

Jim Ludwig's streamlined house slid past, and Frank Keesling's, formerly Ina Claire's. You remember Ina: once the greatest comedienne on the Broadway stage. Then she disappeared into anonymity, or was it the Brocklebank Apartments? Never mind, I knew a drunk once who lived at the Brocklebank but finally had to move. Every time he fell into a cab and mumbled his address, the driver took him to the Crocker Bank.

On Columbus, bumped into Scholer Bangs, who was looking long of tooth and face. You remember Scholer: he was famous once, too—the last of the San Francisco lamplighters, over forty years ago. In the Western Addition dusk, he'd walk along Webster Street between California and Sutter, lighting the street lamps, followed by a horde of kids, many of them kimono-clad, all of them chanting "Limpy, limpy lamplighter, San Francisco flea-biter, when the lamps begin to light, then the fleas begin to bite."

Well, the fleas have disappeared, more or less, and so have the lamplighters. As for Scholer, he lives in Los Angeles now. Hates it. "My first trip back in years," he said. "Got off the cable at the foot of Hyde and couldn't believe my eyes. Real gas lights! I went to the Buena Vista and said, 'Do they have lamplighters, too?' Thought I might get my old job back. 'Hell, no,' he said. 'They leave 'em burning day and night.' And then I felt precisely like what I've become—just another tourist from Los Angeles."

Left him sighing and wheezing, and pressed on toward Kearny. I don't think you could raise a gang there today to topple a statue or set out for the Galápagos, but around Jackson, it's still pretty colorful. Peruvian and Chinese restaurants. Filipino pool halls and barbershops, the barbers sitting in their chairs between customers and playing guitars and violins. The big hotel that was once a whorehouse—two doors from the old Hall of Justice.

Peered through a window into Enrico Banducci's office, above the hungry i. Enrico may not have the most elegant office in town, but it's the most ridiculous: two rolltop desks, a pool table, a billiard table and three phones that never stop ringing.

"Hey, Bandooch," I said, "I'll play you for a buck." "You're on," he said, dumping his secretary off his lap and grabbing a cue, or even vice versa. I broke and began running the table, having learned the art young at my father's knee in Sacramento. A cop walked in, dragging an old Chinese fellow. "Hey, Enrico," said the cop. "Give Wong here a job, he's the best damn janitor in town." "Okay, Monahan," said Enrico, "send him down tonight. With his own mop."

A drunken seaman came in, waving a bottle and dancing around the room. "Hey, Enrico!" he shouted. "I got my papers again—I'm going back to work! I ship out tonight!" "That's wonderful, Kelly," said Enrico, "just wonderful." The seaman pulled the secretary out of her chair and began dancing around with her. I sank the

fifteen in the side pocket and expected Bill Saroyan to walk in any minute. His kind of scene.

A man in PG&E coveralls leaned against the door, silently watching the pool game. At last he asked, "Is Enrico Banducci here?" "He's out of town," said Enrico, chalking his cue. The PG&E man studied Enrico's beret for a while. Then he asked, "Who's in charge here?" "The man in charge will be back at four," said Enrico. "Why?" The PG&E man waved some papers. "I got orders to turn off the lights in the hungry i tonight," he said, shrugging.

Enrico slammed down his cue. "*Now* I'm Enrico Banducci," he said, snatching the papers. "How much do I owe? A lousy $137? You'd cut off a man's juice for a lousy $137?" He grabbed a pen and scribbled a check. The phone rang. "Hungry i," said Enrico. "Who's in the show? Well, madam, there's Dick Gregory and two acts

whose names I can't remember." I sank a three-ball combination. "Lady," he screamed, "do you realize that while you're talking I'm getting *killed*?" He slammed down the phone.

I pocketed my winnings and trudged back to the typewriter. Whose bread I win, his song I sing, and so I sing this song of Enrico Banducci and what's left of life and color on old Kearny Street.

I've been hearing the canard "San Franciscans are smug and complacent" all my life, from smug New Yorkers to complacent Los Angelenos, but why? Everybody I know is worried as hell about everything: war, baldness, peace, high-rise apartments, low-cost housing, the future of unwed sex, bridges, Bridges, bridge tournaments, Vietnam, which Guinea has the crisis, the displacement in martinis caused by oversized olives. Everything.

To bolster my feeling that complacency is the last thing we have to worry about, I called a civic leader at the City Hall. "Are you smug and complacent?" I asked. "Just a minute, I'll look," he said, putting down the phone. He was back in a few seconds. "Absolutely not," he said firmly. "Sallow and dyspeptic, with yellowish circles under the eyes, caused no doubt by fatigue and overwork, but not s. and c."

And so I repeat, this loose talk has got to stop. Just because we have the greatest city in the world, filled with splendid citizens who will face and surmount their problems with the unquenchable spirit that rose phoenix-like from the ashes of disaster, is no reason to call us smug and complacent. The humble pride of natural superiority. It's more like that.

The fearless destroyers of straw men are always on the march. As though by pre-arranged signal—perhaps a sour note on a broken typewriter—the attack has been joined from all directions: national magazines, jealous rivals of San Francisco, and even a gaggle of local hacks.

The straw man, more often than not, is something they call, pejoratively, the "San Francisco myth." Having set it up by complaining they were led to believe that San Francisco is lusty, gusty, brawling, and bawdy, they knock it down with the further complaint that the city is really a vulgar and fraudulent old bore, coming apart at some of the seamiest seams this side of Port Said—Port Said being, of course, another literary myth.

The argument couldn't be more specious, for the plain and simple reason, as Penrod used to remark to Sam, that there is indeed a San Francisco myth, just as there is a Manhattan myth, a London myth, a Chicago myth, a Hollywood myth, a Paris-Vienna-Belgrade myth, and, undoubtedly, a Yuba City legend. As long as people have the imagination and sensitivity to dream of glory, to embellish their lives with heroes real or fancied and to feel a continuity with the past, the myths will live. They are more necessary to a city's soul than rapid transit.

Blessed are the myth-makers, for they make life bigger than life, a remarkable feat in any age. The Easterner who said, in the time of the Gold Rush, that "San Francisco is the city no coward ever set out for, and no weakling ever reached," may have been guilty of hyperbole, but when his florid epigram flashed up and down the muddy streets and through the ramshackle buildings, the new San Franciscans must have felt a surge of pride and, perhaps, their first common bond. A man who had a way with words had summed them up as somehow different, braver, and more noble, and they were able to look at each other—and their hardships—with new eyes.

The legend is almost never rooted in fact, but it doesn't matter. I don't know whether Willie Britt ever said, "I'd rather be a busted lamppost on Battery Street than the Waldorf-Astoria"; all I know is that the words have a fine Western brash-ness and I never walk along Battery Street without recalling them. The man who first said grandly, "There is no such thing as an ex-San Franciscan" could be proved wrong, statistically, a thousand times over; on the other hand, the phrase lives on in the hearts of a thousand San Franciscans who now live elsewhere, and their letters prove it, day after day. Wherever they go, they carry the San Francisco myth with them. Wherever they are, they hear a foghorn at midnight and the clang of a cable, and they feed on the memories that blend softly into legend.

It's no trick at all to put the knock on fables. Those that do call themselves "realists," and to them, the juice of life is as sour as a lemon, or the look on their faces. In New York, there is no Great White Way, nor can they picture a penthouse way up in the sky; it is only dirt and pushy people. Chicago is not that toddlin' town, just ugly and windswept. In Hollywood, the realists have a sure eye for the phoniness, and fail to hear the faintly rustling ghost of the myth that Hollywood itself allowed to die—the myth of glamor and fabulous foolishness that once gave it a place among the golden cities. A myth is highly perishable; once it is killed by careless handling, it is gone forever.

The realist could make a strong case for the premise that Emperor Norton was a nut and a pest who wouldn't be tolerated for a minute by the hard-nosed Montgomery Streeters of today, but the argument would be of no consequence. The wise mythologists made a symbol out of him, a trademark for a kind of warm craziness in the San Francisco spirit that can be killed only by blind intolerance—and "realism." The character known as Oofty-Goofty, who allowed people to hit him as hard as they could (for a fee) might have been as big a pain in the neck as he had pains in the back, but he was the forerunner of Barney Ferguson and Tiny Armstrong and the man who walks up and down Columbus Avenue, blowing his dime-store flute in the authentic tones of eccentricity.

There are those in San Francisco today who, whether they are aware of it or not, are part of the continuing myth. You might know them as egomaniacs, publicity seekers, gold-plated parvenus, or windy old bores, but be not misled. Fifty years hence, if the legend makers are still at their craft, they will have been woven into the tapestry of a glittering pageant—and the San Franciscan of 2012 will read of them with wonderment, and vow to keep the faith.

"But," argues the realist in rebuttal, "San Francisco is full of discrimination, and racists, and hate groups." Only the expansive feeling that created an Emperor Norton can fight that successfully. Can you think of a better reason for the care and feeding of a myth?

I was amused to read, in a recent issue of a national magazine, that "in appearance, San Francisco is not much different from Akron or Kansas City or a dozen other American cities." Poor purblind fellow, so far removed from the poetry and vision that make any city more than a collection of sticks and stones. Compare his leaden words with those of Bret Harte, who saw "Such breadth of sea, such breadth of sky!" Or of George Sterling, who looked up and cried with ecstatic pleasure: "At the end of my streets are stars!" Thus do the dreamers show themselves to be more real than the realists.

San Bruno and first view of city skyline coming from airport

Mission Dolores

NO matter what anybody tells you, it's fun being a tourist. For one thing, you're allowed to look dumb, act dumb, and ask silly questions. When you walk around strange streets with your mouth open, people don't think you have adenoids; they know you're impressed with the sights, and they love you for it. While you might get overcharged in restaurants, you can always undertip, pleading ignorance of the money.

It was in this mood that I returned to San Francisco from a European vacation, looking like any other tourist at the airport. My clothes were wrinkled. My bags, under-eye and hand, were battered and bleeding. When I went to tip my porter, I found I had only Swiss francs in my pocket. "First time in San Francisco?" he inquired. The temptation was too great. "Yup," I said. "Where you from?" he went on. "Uh—Oshkosh, b'gosh," I said.

"You'll like San Francisco," he said pleasantly, picking up my bags. "Very cosmopolitan city." He looked at the Swiss francs in my hand. "Is that Oshamakosh money, or whatever you said?" he asked. I laughed. "No, my good man," I said, "It's Swiss. Now then, where's the foreign exchange counter? I'd like to change this. I imagine tipping is the custom here." "Yes *sir*," he said hastily, "but there's no foreign exchange counter I know of."

"But isn't this supposed to be an international airport?" I demanded. Chalk up one black mark for San Francisco. The porter examined a twenty-franc Swiss note. "Well, it *looks* like money," he said, stuffing it in his pocket. "I'll take a chance on it." The Swiss banks will be delighted to hear this.

In U.S. customs, a deadpan inspector made me open my bags. He rummaged around in my laundry, which made me uncomfortable. What is more personal than your own laundry, especially when it needs laundering? "Look, my man," I said in my direct, Oshkosh way, "they didn't make me open my bags in London, or Nice, or Barcelona, or Zurich, or—" he didn't say anything. He just sort of stared at me. I gazed into the distance and whistled an old Oshkosh folk song. He gave me a final short stare and said, "You can go."

Zipping my bags and my lip, I went over to Passport Control. Before he would stamp my passport, the officer picked up a huge book, turned to the C's, and went through it, to see if I had been barred from the United States for treason, defaulting on my alimony payments, or foot-in-mouth disease.

Eventually he stamped my passport, but I felt definitely intimidated. America wasn't acting as friendly as I had expected. After all, wasn't I one of those huddled messes with wretched refuse that Emma Lazarus had written about?

Still playing the role of tourist, I got into a cab. "You go to San Francisco?" I asked the driver in a heavy Swiss accent. "Why not?" he shrugged, throwing the flag. "Nice airport you got here," I said. "Too small," he grunted. "Everything we build around here is obsolete before it gets off the ground." We passed Bufano's tall, tubular statue of Peace. "What time's the blast-off?" I chuckled heartily. The driver sighed. "Boy, all you tourists make the same joke," he said.

We drove onto a wide highway filled with big cars, each containing only one person going somewhere in a terrible hurry. As we passed a string of factories, I

Midway down Telegraph Hill. Treasure Island in the background

commented, "So this is San Francisco." "Nah," said the driver. "It's South City or San Bruno or something. I'll tell you when we get to Frisco." "Don't call it Frisco," I said automatically. "Frevvinsakes," sputtered the driver, "You know about that 'way over in Switzerland?" "I read a lot," I said, fluttering my eyelids.

A cold-looking bay appeared on our right and we started along a causeway. Scavenging birds formed a gray cloud over an endless garbage dump. A grim-looking structure was visible on the right. "Is that San Quentin?" I inquired. "Candlestick Park," yawned the driver, who was probably tiring of my questions. "That's a funny name," I ventured. "It's a funny place," he said. "They got a funny team called the Giants who play a game called baseball the funniest way you ever saw."

Meanwhile, the meter in the cab was ticking at an insane rate. Every few seconds, it recorded another dime, and, being a thrifty Swiss from Oshkosh, I acted properly startled. When it passed five dollars I was really startled. "Say," I said, "that meter isn't broken, is it?" He got off a short, mirthless laugh. "Brother," he said, "that gadget isn't broken, it's a breaker. It breaks *people*."

A long, impressive skyline appeared in the distance. "That's San Francisco," said the driver briefly. We were now on a freeway of some sort, and the traffic became even more fierce. The driver took a firmer grip on the wheel. "I can't talk much any more," he said. "From now on it's idiots all the way."

I nodded and looked around with the confused eyes of the tourist. A large bridge, which I took to be the Oakland-Golden Gate Bridge, plunged off into the distance. As we inched along a crowded downtown street, I saw a lot of tow-trucks hauling cars away; apparently American cars aren't as efficient as I'd heard. The city looked reasonably clean, but bare. For blocks and blocks, one sees no trees. Just pavement and more pavement.

At the top of Telegraph Hill, I tried to pay the driver off in Swiss francs. "No soap," he said firmly, so I ran to my landlady and borrowed a cup of money. "Thanks, fella," he said, pocketing a tenner. "I hope you enjoy San Francisco." I'm sure I will. Everybody says it's a great town.

Van Ness Avenue dominated by City Hall dome

California Street, past Grace Cathedral to cross Grant Avenue. Bay Bridge, background

Summer in San Francisco is not like summer anywhere else. An icy wind sweeps across Chestnut Street on Russian Hill. Fog, overdrawn from the bank outside the Gate, races across the bay at jet speed, and an eerie half light filters down on a bilious green freighter plowing westward against the incoming tide, a white mustache foaming at her prow.

A summer dusk, but not the summer of ice cream, watermelon, and sweat; the tourist ladies shiver in their cotton dresses and wrap themselves in their arms for warmth. A man wearing a bandoleer of cameras sits at the improvised sidewalk café outside Lefty's saloon, blowing on his hands, his Tom Collins looking as out of place as an astronaut on a cable car.

This is not the summertime of fly swatters, screen doors and rockers on wide porches. The evocative sound of a lawn mower is nowhere to be heard, no children whoop and holler at kick-the-can on the street corners, and the lamps wear a halo of moisture. But there are still touches.

On Larkin, a fire truck, returning from a fire, rolls lazily down the street, its bell clanging occasionally. The sleepiness of summer always seems to hang over a fire truck as it meanders back to its house. In the next apartment, somebody is practicing a Chopin nocturne, playing the same four bars over and over, always making the same mistake, always going back to the beginning.

Chopin has the sound of summer too. You remember tree-shaded streets, all the front doors open, and somebody always practicing Chopin or Mozart—the composer who is too simple for children, too difficult for artists, as Mr. Rubinstein once said.

You drive around the summer city, looking at the cold new buildings, trying to remind yourself it's July. Here and there, amid the chilly glass cubicles that do indeed look like ice trays in a refrigerator, you see a flash of human warmth. In a block on Pine Street some imaginative soul has revived the wooden front of an old apartment house and bedecked it with a canopy emblazoned "Dolphin Square." There is no square within sight and no dolphin within miles, but the picturesque name gives you a lift, all the same—much more than can be said for the concrete pile arising nearby.

Across the intersection, another poet of the paintpots has been at work on an even older apartment house, emblazoned with trefoils and chesty with a be-damned Victorianism, a huge triangular window over its marquee, supported by gilded caryatids. You had to say one thing for the old architects: they went about as far as they could go, and then a step beyond.

It is summer and the cold wind blows. Nothing seems to proliferate except cars, traffic jams, and the bare steel bones that herald the San Francisco of Tomorrow. One "Dolphin Square" suddenly seems more valuable than a dozen square parking lots in the sky. The new buildings are boring, an especial crime in a city that has always been exciting to look at.

Fortunately, there are still people. You can force them into pigeonholes, but they still come out people, not pigeons, and looking different. You have only to walk along Market Street to be grateful that people, unlike the buildings being presented to us, are not uniform. As somebody once observed, how can two eyes, a nose, and a mouth be arranged in so many ways?

No matter what they try to sell you in the slick four-color ads, a city and its people are not always neat and beautiful. A metropolis is a million odds and ends, mainly odd, that can never be filtered through a concrete box and come out all pink and white and smelling of Arpège. We need more life on our streets, not less, more benches on the street corners, more trees and parks, more vendors selling balloons and hot corn and windup toys that don't work when you get them home, but made you laugh at the street corner.

Let the city stay free and wild. Let there be funny old houses for funny young people, and ugly old buildings, bursting with life on Market. When every building on our hills looks like the one next to it, it will no longer be San Francisco—as it will not be San Francisco when everybody looks, dresses, and thinks alike, if at all.

Do as I do or I'll kill you (ban you, fire you, snub you, turn you in to the FBI). Some people would like San Francisco that way. But they're not the people who come up with a Dolphin Square or peddle newspapers in a derby hat or eat a hot dog on Market Street in the cold wind of July—and keep a city warm and alive.

We're more apt to sizzle in October. You sleep with the covers off (remember, in the old days, when people put their sheets in the icebox during the day and slapped them onto the bed at the last minute?). Dressing is the real hang-up, because San Francisco men would rather swelter than switch to Southern California-weight suits, which they don't have anyway. Although a few young men on Montgomery were wearing Bermuda shorts, Louis Lurie was wearing a vest, as usual. But millionaires, as is well known, don't sweat. They perspire a little Chanel No. 5.

At Jack's, the brokers took off their jackets and hung them on the backs of chairs; it was a shock to discover that some of our leading citizens aren't even half safe and don't wear undershirts. The police were in shirt sleeves, exposing what they usually hide under their tunics: bellies. The Muni bus drivers had it better than anybody; they can take their ties off, and did. The firemen were sprinkling each other with hoses.

Market Street at 2 P.M. looked like the main drag of Tombstone, Arizona, almost deserted on the sunny side, bare, sticky, and steamy. It made you realize afresh that we still don't have enough trees. The few pedestrians huddled in whatever shade was available, waiting for *wait* to change to *walk* so they could bolt across the street. Stores that still believe this city is air-conditioned by God instead of General Electric were stifling; you expected the sprinkler system to go on any minute.

Sign on the window of the S.F. Blocking Studio on Sutter: "Closed this afternoon. Too hot to work. Open in the morning." I'm not quite sure what they do in a blocking studio, but whatever it is, it could wait. The Hippo was doing a big

Playland at Ocean Beach, with Seal Rocks to the left

business with its Burger Sundaes: raw hamburgers topped with vanilla ice cream, nuts, kosher pickle, chocolate sauce, and a cherry. If you haven't tried it, knock it. The Plush Doggy on Market was doing well too, and there's a name to set your teeth on edge on a hot day. Plush and doggy just don't go together, unless you're in the cuddly-toy business. Gimme a plush doggy, and hold the mohair.

It was a pretty weird day, even for Smogville North. I walked into "Original Andy" Lacbay's barbershop on Broadway, and there was Original with a sort of beatific look on his face. "I been in business a long time," he was saying, "and nothing as nice as this ever happened to me." What happened was that one of his steady customers, North Beach fellow named Belluomini, had just included Andy in his will. "After he dies," reported Andy dreamily, "the will states that I, and only me, will be allowed to cut his hair and arrange it properly. A barber couldn't get a finer tribute."

And then there was this mouse race. A saloon called the Mouse House opened on O'Farrell, featuring live mice racing along a wooden track mounted on the wall, the mice being named after disc jockeys and columnists and other dead issue. The S.P.C.A. had a man on the scene—a rather ferret-like individual named Arthur Germaine, very dedicated—and he stopped the proceedings after the first race. His mind, sharp as a steel trap, was made up after Disc Jockey Jim Lange dropped the starting gate on one of the mice and killed it. "Boy," said Mr. Germaine, shaking his head, "when they start killing 'em right in front of me, they've had it." He put the dead mouse in his pocket and pattered out.

Walking around the hot streets didn't help much, either. On Fifth between Market and Mission, a hook 'n' ladder came roaring out of the firehouse behind the Old Mint, and as it swung into Fifth, a case of canned milk fell out of it. Ridiculous. Sirens screaming, and all those cans of milk rolling around the street. Reminded me of the time a three-wheeler cop made a fast turn at Geary and Taylor. Too fast. His tricycle turned over. And out of the box on the back tumbled a case of beer. Even the news in the journals was depressing. There was a squib out of Stockton about a man being arrested for drunk driving in a garbage truck. The item filled me with dread. Is Stockton, even, becoming more colorful than San Francisco?

I got into the car and listened to a disc jockey on KFRC. He was telling a pretty funny story, and that depressed me too. Funnier than anything I had. It was about Arthur Fiedler, the maestro of the "Pops" concerts, waving a couple of free tickets at a chambermaid in the Mark Hopkins and asking "Would you like to go to the concert tomorrow night?" Replied the maid after a moment's thought, "Is that the only night you have off?"

I dropped by the Irisher to see Penny Cillin, the stripper. "I'm changing my name," she said. "I'm tired of being an antibiotic." Her new name is Norma Vincent Peal, which, I warned her, was older than the Fiedler story. "You're Irish and you're working at the Irisher," I said, "so why not change it to Strip O'Mycin? Or, to keep it even more germ free, how about Auntie Biotic?"

She looked at me kind of menacingly so I left and went down to a club on

Broadway tunnel near Powell Street

Powell. It was peculiar. San Francisco on a hot night is like a village. All the neighbors had their windows open and the club had its doors open. Artie Samish, the retired lobbyist, was sitting on a wooden bench outside. Inside Edward Kennedy "Duke" Ellington and his orchestra were playing, and the sounds of "Satin Doll" floated up and down the street. Well, I guess no village is quite like that. Ellington on records, maybe, but not in person, with a stout millionaire sitting outside on a bench.

The conversations were weird, too. Mike Wagner overheard two high school kids talking and one said, "I hope I do better this year than last. Last year I got four F's and one D." "Well," said his buddy, "that's what you get for concentrating too hard on one course." And Stanley Diamond overheard these two guys at the bar. First: "No, I'm not married. I only met one girl I'd ever marry and now I wouldn't even marry *her*." Second: "You're lucky. I never met even *one*." First: "Whaddya mean? You're married and you got three kids, haven't you?" Second: "What the hell's *that* got to do with it?"

It was a strange weekend. From Friday night till late Sunday night time seemed to stand still in the blood-hot heat that lay oppressively on the city. Sweat poured off the brows of the hills and dripped down the towers of the Golden Gate Bridge. Buildings gasped for breath through open windows. Even the delicate, crescent moon seemed to be giving off heat, confounding the poets. Who ever hears of the hot light of the moon?

Somewhere the Cold War was being fought by its icy practitioners. Somewhere soldiers were facing each other, fingers itchy on triggers. Somewhere rockets were angled menacingly to the sky and instant disaster was only a button-push away. Somewhere. But not here. San Francisco moved sluggishly through a fantasy of peace, or is the reality even more fantastic? No matter. It was too hot to think anyway.

The American dream—apple pie and ice cream, Home and Mother, and above all Togetherness, together-wise. San Francisco enacted it through the long, steamy days, to the point of caricature. The cars were out, the tops were down, the seats were filled with happy people in bright clothes, smiling, waving, friendly. Lovers walked hand in sticky hand, kids fished off piers, pretty girls frolicked on the Marina Green, and there were enough simple, heart-warming scenes to keep Norman Rockwell busy for the next thousand years.

The bay looked like a big bathtub, filled with toy boats and pieces of white soap, 99 44/100 per cent pure. There was an eerie, resortlike glow about Alcatraz; you could almost imagine gayly striped umbrellas on its terraces, bodies browning on its rocks. A few brave sailboats tiptoed out under the Gate Bridge to frolic in the open water, like daring children playing outside the safe garden walls.

Peace and plenty under the wild October sun. The cars whizzing up El Camino to Bay Meadows Race Track passed a former used-car lot that now advertises "Fallout Shelters and Survival Information," but nobody was stopping. The winners were getting ready to run, just down the road a piece.

A way of life in the city-state of San Francisco, tucked snugly away at the end of the world (or near it) under a reassuring blanket of haze, warm as mother love. The good fun, the good food, the good drinks—and be merry, for tomorrow we die of a hangover, tomorrow we diet, tomorrow the cold fog may come in, tomorrow we may have to think again. . . .

In Belvedere they play tennis, in proper whites, at the edge of the bay. In Belvedere they swim in the muddy lagoon and float around on tiny boats and sit on the spacious wooden sun decks, drinking long drinks and laughing. Late in the afternoon the sky turns pink and Tamalpais broods in the background. In Belvedere you can hear the splashing as a hundred showers are turned on. The lovely people, the beautiful people are getting ready for the next party.

In Burlingame the butlers wear white jackets and serve frosted drinks on silver trays. In Atherton the proper children splash in proper sparkling pools, surrounded by grass that is greener than green. At Stinson Beach they serve you cans of beer out of coffinlike containers filled with ice as pelicans and helicopters fly overhead. At Stinson Beach the children waddle naked on the beach as the surf crashes in, surprisingly rough, long, bottle-green rollers pounding like drumfire.

At Trader Vic's the convening bankers are smiling and hearty in the new image of bankers, mopping their brows and complaining lightly about the prices ("We're just poor bankers, you know," hahaha). At Alexis' Mr. Alexis sits in the air-conditioned chill of his wine cellar, drinking a rare Pommery pink champagne, his Old Georgian face sad as Emil Brueh plays *Kalitka* on his gypsy violin.

At a cocktail party on Jackson Street, the delicate guitar notes of Bola Sete, late of Rio de Janeiro, float out into the velvet-thick air, where they glitter like dewy pearls. At a party in the St. Francis for a new novel, the windows are open and you can see barefoot old men in Union Square, stretched out on newspapers. At a party in a new air-conditioned room at the Fairmont you can feel your damp shirt freezing to your skin. The small talk is as artificial as the temperature.

At the Beaux Arts Ball Peter Salz pays $12,000 for a Marc Chagall painting displayed by Fred Maxwell ($1800 of that will go to the Boys Club). At 3:30 A.M. opera stars Geraint Evans and Graziella Sciutti are wining and trilling at a party given by the Centurians—"On to the Centurians'!" Out of a passing car comes the thrilling voice of Soprano Mary Costa. . . . You remember a scene out of early Evelyn Waugh. "Oh darling, so many *parties*," he said, cradling his head in her lap. "I know," she said sadly, stroking his head. "I know."

Across the Golden Gate Bridge from Marin County to the city

Leaving the city, one drives above Old Fort Scott

The sunset was long and red Sunday night. The rocky hills of Marin turned salmon pink and the blazing windows on Twin Peaks could be seen as far away as Bolinas.

Deep autumn in the cool gray city of legend. At 5 P.M. it is already dark, all the Old Glories gone from the turrets and minarets. The wet sidewalks glisten like mirrors. Far out in the bay a ship moans; in the thin, chill air it sounds startlingly near. The traffic cops are in their yellow-breasted slickers, and on the hills to the south you can see the great loop of Bayshore Freeway, a glacier of headlights frozen in the age of chrome. The traffic signals go through their cycles, in their mindless way, but the cars stand still. A phonograph playing in an empty room, a sea gull wheeling unseen, a wave crashing unheard on the rocks at Lands End.

The city with its coat collar upturned, and a panhandler touching your elbow with a muttered "Cupacawfee?" The sailor snuggles with his pickup on a cable car and whispers "Let's go home someplace"; she giggles, reddens, glances around. On a Chinatown slope, an Oriental child, lovely as a spring blossom, scampers into a cobbled alley where tongmen flashed knives. In the sweatshops, behind drawn shades, a thousand sewing machines are busy; the infinite patience of Chinese ladies, who once went blind embroidering silken treasures.

The city is imperfectly itself in the wintry dusk. The old skyscrapers, lovingly wrought, look like the Suydam drawings in a Dobie book. Elegant city of furs and tatters, perfume and stench, a flutter of wings over the Municipal Dump and a ripple of laughter in a thousand saloons. On Third Street the police paddy wagons (made by International Harvester) are out harvesting cosmopolitan drunks; the sober are standing in line for a churchly handout. Pinched or unpinched, they are all in the same boat, foundering within sight of Harbor Lights.

City of myth and legend, standing at the crossroads, unmoving as the signals flash red for danger and green for where do we go from here? Pass the buck, make a buck, and raise high the roof beam, carpenter, the rents are going higher yet. Cab-riding tourists scream on the slippery hills, women scream in the psychiatric ward at S.F. General, and the pigeons in the square and the squirrels in the park are getting fatter than ever; never have there been so many people to feed them. In the Tender-loin cafeterias, the mirrored walls multiplying solitude into infinity.

The November city, on the brink of the happy holidays. A friendless girl kills herself in her tiny hotel room, and the mailboxes are stuffed with gift brochures. November, the month for nostalgics. Family reunions, class reunions, "You haven't changed a bit too much," "To think I almost married *that*," and the Big Game; let us now praise famous men like Pesky Sprott, Cort Majors, Andy Smith, and Brodie Stephens. The old Big Game nights, when the hotels had to strip their lobbies bare (or the rioters would do it for them) and you went dancin' with Anson with a bottle of rotgut concealed in your girl's corsage box. Young Herbie Fleish-hacker drove a Stutz Bearcat, and the world was young and rich. A mountain of old gardenias, turning brown at the edges and smelling like a sickroom.

November night, the new scarecrow buildings cluttering up the skyline, cubes for squares, the boxes that computers come in. "Breathtaking view!" at a price that takes your breath away and at a cost of somebody else's view. Vistas without vision, and give us this day our daily breadth. Anything you can build I can build higher. Sir, I find your altitude highly offensive, and the little home in the West is now $90,000. November in the enchanted city, and the filled busses snort along.

The great game of December. You don't need a calendar to know it's December. You can feel it and smell it and hear it wherever you wander along the downtown streets. Hot mink and warm perfume in the jam-packed stores, wet noses and dry gin in the crowded bars—and the tinkling of many bells, manned by the scrubbed girls in Salvation Army blue, gazing at you evenly through steel-rimmed glasses. And somehow, because you've got that kind of monkey mind, you remember the house of joy that was padlocked in North Beach many a wrong year ago, where-upon the madam, more whimsical than most, tacked a little sign over the buzzer. It read "Belle Not Working."

December, the season to be jolly and jowlly, with many a ho-ho-ho from the mechanical Santa Clauses (and where was the store that advertised "Five Santas— No Waiting"?). Even the traffic cops look cheerier, with their beet-red faces, even though the color was applied by the weather, or maybe a much-needed nip at the corner saloon (the December traffic would drive any right-minded cop to drink).

And meanwhile, under the dark skies (the lights come on early, as in the fourth quarter of a football game), the signals blink red and green, the colors of Christmas—red for your bank account, green for your face when you open the bills.

The December town—fun to walk around in, for the people are out, under the rain that pelts the pelts on the fine ladies and makes a damp crisis out of your damn creases. And even when the sun comes out, it is cold and far away, as though it were turning its face to a more distant sun. On Market Street the armies march to and fro, armies of strangers rubbing elbows, carrying umbrellas like weapons and bundles like treasures under their arms—a wonderful cross-section of cross-faced people bringing joy to the world, somebody's world, on Christmas morn.

Downtown—how nice there's still a downtown, as the shopping centers and the nifti-thrifti marts go marching on across the faraway hills of upper suburbia and Lower Slobovia. Downtown: it has a nice, dated sound and a nice dated look, a few mad blocks of excellent shops and beautiful windows and the age-old department-store scene of flying elbows around a bargain counter. You look up and almost expect to see the wire baskets whizzing past on overhead trolleys as they did forty years ago, carrying change to the cashier, and the old lady salesgirls with their yellow pencils stuck in their hair, fluffed out with rats, and their pince-nez dangling from their shirtwaists on fine gold chains. And the tacky little Tenderloin bars, each with a wreath in the window and a little sign announcing "Tom 'n' Jerries"—so sad with yestertears. Who drinks Tom 'n' Jerries in this age of scotch and vodkatinis? Butter me no rum, batter me no eggnogs.

You shop, look, and listen through the precious few streets, drinking in the seasonal sights, the good will and ill—and under all the grabbing and griping, there is an unmistakable feeling of peace in the air (the rockets seem as far away as they should be, and certainly the world won't erupt until the January white sales, at least). The schoolgirls, all giggly cute in their canvas coats on the cable cars, their bundles mixed in with their books. The inevitable shopping sight: the little woman struggling with a package as big as she, her strapping husband carrying a tiny bag daintily between thumb and forefinger. And a chuckle at Geary and Stockton: the sidewalk photographer trying to take a picture of an oncoming little old lady—and she waving her umbrella angrily and snapping at him, "Don't you dare! Why, I've lived here all my life!"

You lounge around in a toy shop on Post, feeling a slight chill as you watch the activity around an amazingly lifelike doll called "Baby Dear," made of soft rubber that feels eerily like skin. One by one, furtively, the lonely old women sidle up to Baby Dear and cradle her in their arms, cooing and fussing and rubbing their hands over the soft surface. Sighs a clerk, "One woman came in here four or five times to play with a Baby Dear. We knew what she was going to do, and we all turned our backs. Sure enough, she finally grabbed one and clutched it to her—just like a real child—and ran out the door. I hope it makes her Christmas."

The lonely and the homeless—they're the ones that reach you while the December bells are ringing. And yet, over on Skid Road, past the pawnshops and the sodden hotels with the signs that warn "No Drunks," you always seem to find one pan-

Fisherman's Wharf at the foot of Taylor Street

handler with the spirit unquenchable. Such a one walked up to Fireman Paul Paulbitski, in front of Truck 13 on Drumm Street, and showed fifteen cents in his palm. "Hey, fireman, wanna make that an even quarter?" he said jauntily. Paul fished up a dime and dropped it in his hand. "Got any kids?" the Skidrowgue asked. "Two," said Paul. The bum fished around in a pocket and extracted two pennies. "Here," he said, dropping them in Paul's shirt pocket, "put those in their piggy bank for Christmas." Merry Christmas to you, old man.

I try to be one of the first few thousand people out looking for spring. I don't always choose the right day. One that comes to mind was definitely wrong. The skies were as gray as November's. The cable car slots lay silent—it was as though the city had lost its voice. The turntable at Powell and Market stood empty, and a tourist with a camera around his neck and a kid clutching his hand kept asking: "Where'd they go? What happened?" The kid looked like he might cry any minute.

On Eddy, discarded newspapers fluttered in an icy wind. The headlines in the gutter told of death in Vietnam, of escalation by frustration. The same papers were also announcing that spring was here, and the condition of Orlando Cepeda's knee rated as much ink as a helicopter shot down in the jungle.

I turned up the collar on my trenchcoat, whispering "Here, spring, pretty spring, where are you, spring?" Nothing crossed my path but black cats, pigeons, and other strange birds, the latter wearing tight pants and high heeled boots. Wither and wither the flowers of spring? A few anemic geraniums shivered in tin cans on the window ledges of cheap rooming houses. The only fruit was the neon cherry in the neon cocktail glass on the signs outside a saloon. A few broken blossoms drifted past: pasty-faced B-girls with kerchiefs over the rollers in their hair.

It had to be somewhere, I slid behind the wheel of my half-Aston-Martin, lit the wrong end of a cigarette and drummed my fingers on the horn button. If I were spring, where would I hide? Of course! I slid up through the gears, flinching only slightly, and headed for Marin.

The great red bridge lay cold and gaunt, arching its back toward green hills. I smiled my way through the toll plaza, forcing a quarter tip on the collector, and looked at the bay below—a bowl of angry gray suds churning against the rocky cliffs of Alcatraz.

It was warmer in Marin. Spring was more than a rumor. I drove slowly through the quiet streets of Mill Valley, but I was too late. Spring had already been there. You could tell by the lush lawns and the leafy trees. Kids were throwing baseballs and tantrums; here and there you could hear the tinkle of glass as a ball crashed through a window. A good sound, as nostalgic as summer in a small town.

I droned through a warm valley toward Olema. Fat, lumpy cows dotted the hillsides, getting homogenized, or whatever it is they do. Boys were fishing in rushing streams. The smoke from a hundred barbecues rose from Sam Taylor State Park. Spring could have been hiding anywhere. Kids fishing, a wonderful sight: I smiled dreamily and reminisced about fishing with a throw line in the muddy Sacramento, catching nothing but hell for coming home late.

Tomales Bay, and cooler again—the trail of Spring growing cold. I stopped at a Czech restaurant and ate some Tomales Bay oysters bordelaise and drank a bottle of Montrachet. The young headwaiter wore a proper dark suit, batwing collar, and black bow tie. In Marin, he looked a little out of place, even a little out of date. Or, in the age of drive-ins and sport shirts, are all the niceties out of date?

I drove back toward the city, past the cows homogenizing on the hills.

At Fisherman's Wharf, the people were bundled up against the biting wind. It was so cold the crabs were fighting to be thrown into the boiling water. Little old ladies sat pinch-faced on wooden benches, spooning crab meat out of paper cups. There was a smell of salt in the air, and fish and rust and hemp and catsup, mingling in an awful and wonderful way.

I walked along the block above the wharf, where a halfhearted carnival atmosphere warmed the air slightly. People drinking mugs of coffee at a few sidewalk tables. A *Hof brau* kind of place, featuring an accordionist wearing a Tyrolean hat and lederhosen. A saloon at the corner was offering near-naked dancers, their excellent bodies covered with gold paint. The late Ian Fleming would have been amused.

North Beach on Sunday night. What's the Italian word for *gemütlich? Simpatico?* Anyway, the feeling is there, no matter what the temperature, no matter how loud the screams about sin, smut, and corruption. North Beach on Sunday night is still the close-knit families going out for dinner, in their Sunday best, and the smell of wine, tomato sauce, and Parmesan.

I dropped in at the Gold Spike, one of the good old places. A Gigli record was playing on the jukebox something from *Rigoletto*. A bartender with a good, solid face, making good, solid drinks for four bits. Checkered oilcloths on the tables.

I sank into a booth and went through the traditional works—the typical North Beach Italian family dinner, its routine unvaried through the year of ceaseless change. The dish of salami, olives, and peppers, the basket of sour-dough. The big bowl of excellent minestrone, the lettuce and tomatoes with the oil and vinegar. The platter of ravioli—"homemade," the waitress said, as usual—and as usual, great. Chicken and string beans, coffee, the dish of sweet Italian cookies. All that for $2.85, plus wine. Nice.

I drove home through the rain, the wipers wigwagging on the windshield. The tall buildings reached up to puncture the storm clouds that lay darkly on the hills. Maybe spring will be a little late this year. Or maybe it has been and gone. In San Francisco, you never know.

For six days of the week San Francisco is a city in a groove. On the seventh it explodes into a dozen Sundays.

There is the picture-postcard Sunday . . . a yacht-dotted bay . . . a silhouette of a Lincoln Park golfer against the red exclamation marks of the Golden Gate Bridge . . . squat Harbor Cruise boats, flirting among the rocks of Alcatraz (but daring to go closer now).

Golden Gate Park

Sunday is a kid self-conscious in his first pair of baseball spikes, clumping along the pavement to a game at Potrero Hill Playground . . . a Sunset District family washing the car, young mother wearing a raincoat over her Bermudas . . . the motliest of all throngs at Playland, drifting unsmiling past the insane recorded laughter at the Fun House (Joyless-at-the-Beach) . . . the smell of expensive sweat around the bar at the California Tennis Club, waiting impatiently for Bartender Ken Matsuhiro's impossible-to-duplicate orange frappés. Car-trapped tourists bottle-necked on the curving road to Coit Tower, waiters obligingly photographing tourists on the deck of The Trident, night people behind dark glasses at Enrico's Caffeine Society, overcoated Mittel-Europeans eating the meat blintzes at David's Delicatessen, Chinese families peeling pork-filled buns at the Hang Ah Tea Room.

Sunday is a flowered hat on the way to church, a laughing crowd on a cable car, and an old man asleep on a bench in Golden Gate Park, and so much more.

Mr. and Mrs. San Francisco are drawn irresistibly to the sea on a sunny Sunday. They drive in droves through the park, straining for that first glimpse of the water. They spread out along the beach, they cluster in the Cliff House, they stare at Seal Rocks with anguished eyes as though they wish they could frolic there too. They range along the Marina and look at the sails and lose themselves in Mitty-like dreams of galleons and doubloons along the Spanish Main. For San Franciscans, all of them—the clerks, the housewives, the bookies, the bankers—are sprinkled ever so slightly with salt spray, and on Sunday they go down to the sea in cars to fill their lungs with the tang of their heritage.

Candlestick Park

Sunday is a drive to a ball game. A favorite subject for San Francisco wits is the city's professional football team, the 49ers, the only team in the league that has never won a championship. "They are called the 49ers," it has been observed, "because they never cross the 49-yard line." They perform in an obsolete stadium called Kezar, which is also unique. It is perhaps the only stadium in big-time football that runs east and west, for a very San Francisco reason. It is in Golden Gate Park, whose longtime overseer, the late John McLaren, didn't want it there in the first place. He finally agreed, reluctantly, when the city said it would build the stadium east and west. If it had been built in the traditional manner—running north and south—it would have destroyed one of McLaren's favorite petunia beds, and that was where he drew the line.

When the New York Giants moved to San Francisco, there was more fun for all, especially when its home, Candlestick Park, was built on the outskirts of town, in a bleak, windswept area near Hunters Point. The park is so cold, cheerless, and uncomfortable that its architect, John Bolles, the designer of many distinguished buildings, came under an immediate torrent of abuse. Sports writer Charles Einstein rose to his defense with a sensible remark. "Don't be too hard on him," he advised. "After all, it was his first ball park."

Nevertheless, the wags had a field day, calling it everything from "Candlesick" to "The Cave of Winds" and the "Polar Grounds," this last being a fair pun on the Giants' old New York home, the Polo Grounds. Another drawback is that the parking lot is situated well below the stadium, and the steep rise that has to be climbed became known immediately as "Cardiac Hill." So many fans died of heart attacks while scaling these heights that someone thought the name of Candlestick Park should be changed to Memorial Stadium.

Many crusty old San Franciscans—the kind who rejoice in the city's near-isolation from mainland U.S.A. and, indeed, from reality—looked with misgivings on the arrival of the baseball mercenaries, especially when the newspaper headlines brayed: "S.F. Goes Major!" Typical retort: "They mean the National League has gone major by joining San Francisco." Nevertheless, the fans responded in record-breaking numbers, and some of them turned out to be strictly bush: during the first couple of seasons, they actually booed the immortal Willie Mays, apparently for not hitting a home run every time he came to bat. The New York writers were amazed and disgusted, especially a contingent that happened to be in San Francisco at the time of Nikita Khrushchev's visit (the then-Russian dictator was warmly received). "What a town," wrote a bewildered Frank Conniff of New York. "They cheer Khrushchev and boo Willie Mays!"

However, in the intervening years, the San Francisco baseball devotee has come of age. He and Willie Mays now have a warm regard for each other, and, when the team blows a game or a pennant, the catcalls no longer ring out in San Quentin South, another term of affection for Candlestick Park. The San Francisco fan now more closely resembles the typical old-time New York Giant fan, of whom an unknown author once wrote:

"He is male, and getting old. He never waits till next year, because he expects

Hunters Point on way from city to airport. Left to right: Navy Yard,
Candlestick Park, railraod yard, and part of Cow Palace at extreme right

nothing. He can be hurt, but never disappointed, and he wears his hurt in a quiet sort of way.

"He is the kind of guy who invariably sticks his finger in the coin-return slot of a pay phone after he hangs up. He knows there won't be any money there. He is merely playing the percentage.

"He never goes to a ball game at any park except the Giants' park. He refers to his Giants only by their last names (Dodger fans use first names. Yankee fans use phrases: 'The Big Guy,' 'The Left Fielder').

"His memories are equal in defeat and victory. He remembers not the occasion, but the incident, the man. He remembers Ott sticking that foot up in the air, and Hubbell pitching on a dark day, McGraw storming at the umpire and Matty's fadeaway.

"Defeat on the ball field is part of his philosophy. He runs into the same thing with his wife, his boss, the bus driver, and the ticket-taker. He never argues. Not the Giant fan.

"He broods. He sits and watches and broods some more. But he comes out and watches the Giants. For he knows, down deep, that someday they will make it. It figures on percentage."

The San Francisco Giant fan hasn't quite achieved this quiet desperation, this nobility of soul. He still feels that next year might be the year of the money in the coin-return slot. But the feeling is fading fast.

There's more to Sunday in the city than the weekly traffic jam caused by people with a single thought in thousands of automobiles. And in my own perverse way I like the other side of the picture—where time stands still in the hush of a deserted street.

I enjoy the Sabbath silence of the financial district, noisy with a new dimension of unpeopled space. Along the empty sidewalks only vagrant scraps of paper scud before the wind that, on other days, toys with men's hats and women's skirts. The imposing skyscrapers suddenly look lost and childish without the people who make them tick between long weekends. What is more useless than a skyscraper on Sunday?

Sunday is quiet and kindly on the Embarcadero. The big ships doze at the ends of their lines, as though the water were tepid enough to make them sleepy. The saloons are empty and the bartenders stand outside the doors, talking to children. Only the Ferry Building seems unaware that this is the Sabbath; every day is Sunday now, for this sad old pile of gray—dead and useless except for the clock that goes ticking on when all else is gone.

Along O'Farrell, Eddy, and Ellis the pasty-faced people who are chained to tiny apartments venture out to the sidewalks, like prisoners at the ends of their short ropes. From their kitchenettes they drag little white chairs, and there they sit in the sun, close to their front doors, as though they might have to dart back into their holes at a moment's notice. The oldsters squat on the stone stairs, blinking and uncomfortable, and gaze down at the warm pavement, for deep inisde they know the sun is only for the rich.

Only in Fillmore's "Little Harlem" are the sidewalks teeming with people in their Sunday best and worst, lounging, talking, standing in busy knots. A tenement is bad enough during the week, but on a sunny Sunday it is unbearable.

Sunday in the far reaches of the Mission and Visitacion Valley and Butchertown has a special flavor—not of San Francisco, but of any small town in any era of the American story. On street corners and between houses the kids lazily throw a baseball while little girls in pink dresses watch from their porches and follow the flight of the ball, back and forth, back and forth. In the distance you can hear the oddly nostalgic clatter of a lawn mower. Under a shade tree a man and his wife are washing their ten-year-old car until it gleams. A boy on a reluctant bike moves past in a dream. The only thing missing is the bang of a screen door, and your ears strain for it until you remember: there are few flies in San Francisco.

Here and there on the Mission hillsides you see the old houses that stand as mirrors for your memory. The shingled roofs, the plate-glass window that marks the "front" room, the wide porch where ghosts sit and rock in wicker chairs, the brick chimneys—monuments, all, in today's cemetery of white stucco cubicles.

And, suddenly you remember with a strange sharpness the old, unhurried days, when these houses were fresh and new. When there were wide-open spaces for more houses you thought would never come to crowd you in. When the peace and quiet of a Sunday didn't come just once or twice in a year of weeks—but seemed to hang heavy and sweet over the world every day.

The Sunday San Franciscan likes to look at his own city, as though to remind himself of his singular good fortune. He sprawls on the Marina Green and gazes up at the broadly expensive windows of the Heights. If he lives on a hill, he travels to the next one to gaze back at his own eminence. Sometimes he simply drives to Marin's Vista Point to stare across the bay at the most beautiful of all upthrusting profiles—an admiring tourist in his own home town.

One Sunday we went out in search of new views—up and down the bare, sleeping streets where Sunday is a silence. South of Market, the vast warehouses drowsed in the sun, and cats prowled the alleys. In the Deep Mission, the sidewalks were deserted—a feeling of Ghost Town. Out along Third, a smell of fried chicken and a glimpse of people in their Sunday best, chatting on the corners: Sunday afternoon in the Deep South.

On Potrero Hill, little wooden houses lean on each other. The streets are dusty and empty, stretching to infinity in a nightmare version of Midwestern melancholy. Here and there, over garage doors, a horseshoe nailed to a wooden wall, the ultimate small-town touch. In the distance, the towers of finance shimmer like a mirage.

On Geary, you needed no calendar to tell you it was Sunday. The saloons had their doors propped open—and you were not surprised to see lonely old ladies inside, nursing a beer. Sailors and the girls they had picked up the night before stood indecisively at street corners. Why is it you always look at sailors and their girls, never at soldiers and girls?

The Embarcadero Freeway looming over another aspect of Telegraph Hill

As dusk began to cloud the hills, we drove into the past that lives in a long, dreamy circle around Buena Vista Park. Trees and lawns, fringing the old houses that were built in a marvelous excess of loving detail—in an age when there was time. The architects of that era designed you a fantastic conglomeration of pilasters and pediments, cupolas and crenelations, balconies and balusters, and as the cardboard cartons proliferate on all sides, they become even more remarkable to look upon.

At the crest of the park, what is left of the old city spreads around you. By choosing your outlook with care, you can see the City That Was—one of the most innocent forms of self-delusion. The gabled roofs rise redly on the nearby slopes. The treetops of Golden Gate Park march solidly to the sea. The Farallones rise on the horizon, Everest-tall. A freighter inches toward the long, welcoming arm of the Marin shore, far beyond the timeless twin towers of St. Ignatius.

Sunday is where you find it, and here, in the green hush of Buena Vista Park, we found a very special Sunday—far from the blank walls that are rising too fast at the end of our streets.

I do a lot of driving in the city. With raw nerve ends hanging out the window to dry, I drive bumper-to-bumper along Post Street. On occasion, hoping to experience the thrill of the Open Road, I whizz (at all of forty-nine miles per hour) along the Embarcadero Freeway, wondering why it is so short and never failing to murmur "Sorry" as I pass the Ferry Building.

In an exploratory mood, I drive up tortuous Portola through a battery of stoplights, finally achieving the crest of Twin Peaks; there, I gaze out over the beguiling city and look with sad approval at the few remaining patches of open space, already seeming to shrink before an imaginary power shovel.

On Sunday I am likely to be found driving a smart nine miles per hour through Golden Gate Park, just another unit on a conveyor belt of cars, remembering the dear days of yesteryore when the Main Drive was exuberantly alive with open carriages and young men in tight pants riding bicycles, their legs angled out as impossibly as a grasshopper's.

Or, searching for the "feel" of the elusive city, I will roll slowly through the endless weathered wooden blocks of the Far Mission District, where the clocks seem to tick more slowly, or cruise past denuded reaches of the Western Addition, noting with interest that green weeds are beginning to grow softly over the ruins, as they did *(mirabile dictu)* in bomb-wracked London—Nature being a tough old dame.

But most of the time, even as you, I am idling, stomach knotted, at some downtown intersection, waiting for a stream of cars to part like the Red Sea to let me through. What I'm trying to say, at unconscionable length, is that I do a lot of driving in San Francisco. And I would like to say further that the driving is getting worse all the time.

City drivers are not like country drivers. I have an idealized picture of the latter, conditioned by years of car ads and oil company billboards. The country driver is really Driving. Lips drawn back into the *risus sardonicus* by the onrushing wind, he is racing free as a bird down an otherwise empty highway, his powerful engine purring like a well-oiled cat. His hair, of which he has a plethora, is tousled in a manly way (although he is wearing an Ascot, this is not to be construed as a sign that he is necessarily odd and Pebble Beachy).

The companion at his side is, of course, a blonde of mathematically even features, wearing cashmere and the ecstatic look of a girl who is having her fingers nibbled by Marcello Mastroianni. It is a lovely picture and I believe every facet of it.

The city driver on the other hand, is mean and wolflike. He lives a hard life, and he looks it. His beady little eyes dart this way and that, looking for any small advantage. Every other driver is his sworn enemy, to be challenged at each cross street. Using his bumpers as D'Artagnan used his rapier, he feints with feral grace, forward, back, then forward again, victory being achieved—"*Touché!*"—when the other chickens out and lets him pass.

On the prowl for a parking space, he is like a tigress stalking a snack for her young. Deaf to the threatening honks behind him, he inches down the street, shoulders hunched, his knuckles showing white on the wheel, his eyes narrowed and

Down from Broadway to Nob Hill. The towers of Montgomery Street, the Mark Hopkins and the Fairmont Hotels dwarf the Barbary Coast in foreground

menacing. And when he spots a space, he is ready to fight to the death for it. First he swings in and out of the spot to stake his claim. His back-up lights flash fire. He blasts his horn, half in exultation, half in challenge. With spastic gestures he waves the other cars around him. And when finally he has backed into God's little acre, after creasing the fender of the car parked in front and denting the license plate of the one in back, he has to sit there for a moment, completely spent.

San Franciscans are the best and worst drivers in the world. At negotiating the hills fearlessly and furiously, with a pathetic faith in their brakes and reflexes, they show the daring of a Stirling Moss in the *Mille Miglia*. Their manners (and mine), however, are those of twelve children upon being confronted with a very small birthday cake.

They drive as though nobody else were on the street. They turn when they feel like it, without signal. They make nonstop U-turns, looking surprised and a little angry when they're honked at. They drive with their windows up, to be sure they will not disgrace themselves by signaling. The old out-and-down signal, to signify a stop, has disappeared from their lexicon—and it is inevitable that future generations will be born without left arms. Thanks to automatic shifting, the left leg is already doomed.

We have the whole awful array: the parannoyed who gives you the horn while the light is still red; the schizoid who can't make up his two minds and therefore straddles the white line; the confused liberal who starts out in the center lane and gradually veers to the left; the antisocial double-parker who revels in the distress he is causing behind him; and, worst of all, the women, who spend so much time lighting cigarettes and looking at themselves in the rear-view mirror that they shouldn't be allowed at the wheel at all.

Next time, try the bus? Unthinkable! This is a free country, ain't it?—and damn it, stay away from that parking space. I *saw* it first.

The San Franciscan, eternally and infernally preoccupied with his own world, is like city people everywhere. Sometimes he forgets that other worlds exist, right at his doorstep (how often does the Manhattanite visit Brooklyn?). San Francisco has no Brooklyn, with its fading legends of the Trolley Dodgers, the banks of the Gowanus, and the tree that grew, but it does have Oakland, which moves in mysterious ways all its own. So mysterious, in fact, that when the San Franciscan does bestir himself to pay a visit he feels like a character in early Ian Fleming or late John Le Carré. It was in just such a cloak-and-dagger mood that I set out one day....

Putting on a dirty trench coat and arming myself with false identity papers, I crossed the bridge to the Eastern sector. It was cold and rainy, but the chill I felt was caused by more than the weather. What was life really like in the Free Democratic People's Republic of Oakland? Talk had filtered through to the West that they were making great strides over there, catching up fast. I had to find out.

I negotiated the bridge safely—the artificial barrier over which so many had made their escape. The guard at the border was uniformed and grim. I handed over my quarter and whispered "How much to get out again?" He looked at me strangely and didn't answer, but it wouldn't be fair to say he was downright unfriendly. The important thing is to keep in contact with these people.

The first thing I noticed is that there aren't as many lights in Oakland as there are in San Francisco; however, it must be remembered that San Francisco is the West's showcase. There were few shoppers on the street, perhaps because the stores were closed. The people were drably dressed in undistinguished raincoats. Perhaps because it was raining. Who knows? My job was only to observe. I leave the evaluation to those better qualified.

I drove up San Pablo Avenue to a place called Trader Vic's. As is typical in so-called People's Republics, Oaklanders claim to have invented it; the more nationalistic among them insist the West's Trader Vic's is a copy. A man named Joe, guarding the door, asked suspiciously, "May I see your visa?" The food and drinks were good, even by Western standards. The natives at the bar were friendly, but aloof. They stared at my shoes. They can always tell a foreigner by his shoes.

"Trader Vic started here, you know," said a fat man drinking an exotic Eastern drink. He was smiling but his eyes were cold. I decided to play it just as cool. "So I've heard," I said noncommittally. "Yep," he went on, "this was the old Trader's home base. If it weren't for us, he'd never have got going."

I refused to be drawn into the argument. Next he'd be claiming that the branches were satellites, clamoring silently for liberation. I knew the dialectical argument well, having read it in a thousand fortune cookies dropped on the West. "Good night," I said mysteriously.

I called a cab, a reasonable copy of the West's Yellow type, and asked for the Oakland Auditorium Theater. I was on edge, for the moment of truth was approaching: was the Oakland Symphony Orchestra really catching up with our own? Were their people as cultured as ours? Would pianist Glenn Gould really play Beethoven's Fourth? These were the thoughts that hounded me as we drove along the rain-slick streets.

"Is it far?" I asked the driver. "I'm a stranger here." He looked at me with some interest. "Are you from—over there?" he asked. I nodded guardedly, wondering what his reaction would be. "How're things—over there?" he went on. "Fine," I said. "How are things—over here?" He squinted through the windshield. "Can't complain," he shrugged. I understood. There was a two-way radio in the car and he couldn't afford to talk too much in a city with only one daily newspaper and that one tightly controlled.

At the Auditorium Theater, my worst fears were realized. Every seat was taken and there were standees. Some of the women were wearing furs. The theater itself is old-fashioned but it has a certain charm; a remnant of the glorious past. Outside there were lawns and trees—a People's Democratic Park—but nothing to compare with our Civic Center fountain.

The orchestra, under a bushy-haired young man named Gerhard Samuel, sounded polished and professional in Handel and Stravinsky. The Russian again.

A most famous view from Twin Peaks

A stout woman in a cloth coat, seated next to me, said, "I don't know what I'm doing here, I've been sick all day." I studied her sympathetically, but she seemed too big to smuggle to the West. Glenn Gould played the Beethoven and the people cheered and cheered, standing up in tribute. Again, the orchestra had performed nobly.

In the lobby, I literally rubbed elbows with the people. I evaluated them carefully. They seemed to be divided into two groups, male and female. They smoked cigarettes and talked animatedly about the music. Obviously they didn't dare discuss politics. In the crowd I recognized several professors who had crossed the northern border from the notorious Berkeley hotbed. I scribbled their names on a scrap of paper and swallowed it. No telling when it would come in handy.

Gloomily, I took a cab back to my car and headed for the border. I dreaded the morning, when I would have to report to my superiors that Oakland indeed has a first-rate orchestra and crowds every bit as appreciative as ours.

At the border, I handed over another quarter to the guard. No doubt of it, they were making it tough for us to go back and forth. Gritting my teeth, I recrossed the bridge, the sound of that full, lush Oakland string section still ringing in my ears.

Soon the lights of the West were shining through the mist. I was safely home again, but I knew I was not the same man who had set out, almost lightheartedly, so many hours before. While it is too soon to say that we are falling behind—their French horns had, after all, made several mistakes—the time for complacency is past.

As New York is not the United States, San Francisco is not California. This is a stuffy way of saying the obvious: for all its Spanish heritage, San Francisco is very much a city of the world. You could pick it up and set it down almost anywhere, and it would get along without much loss of poise or purpose.

The San Franciscan, gloriously insular on his peninsula, doesn't think much about California. Oh, he is aware it is there—a large and fairly nonsensical state, bordering on insanity, Nevada, and the boundaries of Baghdad-by-the-Bay.

What he has read about California doesn't pique his curiosity unduly. From the newspapers he gathers it is a state short on water and long on invaders from the Midwest. Its largest city, he hears with a certain detachment, is situated in a large basin filled with nuts stewing in smog. Its virgin forests, he reads further, are being defoliated, the waters are polluted, and the blessed land is being defiled by builders with one-tract minds. San Franciscans are content to stay at home, smug and secure in their own cool world. However, thinking nothing ventured, nothing lost, we paid a short visit to California one weekend. Highly educational.

California proper begins just south of Palo Alto, where it turns into a substate called San Jose, which is suffering from the dread Los Angeles syndrome. You can drive for miles and still be in San Jose, your eyes entranced by the sight of overpasses and automobile graveyards. Morgan Hill and Gilroy are more in the tradition of the Old West: long main streets speckled with such romantic names as

Lerner's, Karl's, Rexall, Kress and Bank of America, not to mention Frosty stands.

It is somewhere south of Gilroy how's that for a movie title?—that the cars, having inched along bumper to bumper, begin boiling over. One by one they limp over to the roadside to die. With their hoods raised, they look like prehistoric animals in mortal agony. Nevertheless, the drivers bravely stick their heads into those gaping mouths, and more than one driver has disappeared forever.

Deep into the valleys of deathly heat, the land of corduroy hills, huge trucks, and roadside cafés featuring "Good Eats 24 Hrs." The language is different. Stands offer "Cots" and "Chokes" and "Cukes." Restaurants specialize in "Chickin 'n' Biskits." Cows pick disconsolately at dry stubble. Heat rises in waves from the far-off jagged peaks. "California," announces a billboard, "supplies 43 per cent of the Nation's produce." About 42 per cent of it seems to be on sale along the highway.

We turned off 101 toward Hollister and San Juan Bautista. The tract builders haven't gotten here yet, and the land ranges far and free. This is Joaquín Murietta country; the lean, weather-beaten men in the cowboy boots still walk the sidewalks. Apricots perfume the air and the rancheros sit around their pools and talk about the water and labor shortage and the gophers that are forever chewing at the roots of existence. The war is constant. Men sit around with loaded shotguns across their knees, waiting for a gopher to stick its perky little head out of its hole. Powww. There goes another gopher.

San Juan Bautista is a delightful little town, worth the trip to California. In the streets around the grassy old plaza you can still hear the ghostly rattle of long-gone stagecoaches, and in the bar of the beautifully restored Plaza Hotel the old pool and poker tables are ready for the sharpers that will never come again. Tourists wander through the gloomy old mission, and then head for Louis Benoist's airy white pavilion for three samples of chilled Pinot Chardonnay. Nearby, two good restaurants—Cademartori's and the Casa Rosa—and a main street waiting for a gun fight.

I'm not a complete illiterate about the euphoric state I love. I know Tahoe to be a gorgeous lake almost completely surrounded by avarice. Aptos is an enchanted community, so ingrown it borders on incestuousness. Santa Cruz has its head in the sand and its tail in the past. Monterey is famous for Gallatin's and the ghost of Cannery Row, Carmel is trapped between Old Quainty-Waintsy and Supermarket Slick, and you can't get into Pebble Beach unless you know the password, which is "Sam sent me."

As for everything south of the Tehachapis, it reminds me of those ancient maps of a flat world, whose waters are boiling over the edges into Terra Incognita, the pre-Columbian name for Los Angeles. If it weren't for the Los Angeles area, this wouldn't be the most populous state in the union. Think about it. On the other hand, forget it.

California is all things to all people, he said sententiously. There are those who love the great Central Valley, but it's hot at night and there's nothing to do in the daytime unless you dig fruit and vegetables (I do, I do!). I've only seen Mount Whitney from the air, and thanks to every pilot who flies over it, I know that it's not only one of the highest spots in the nation, it's next to Death Valley, which is the lowest, if you don't count the birch groves of Orange County.

Nevertheless, it's the grandest state of all, as the old song would have it, and I'm only sorry I didn't get to know it better before it became overrun to the point of running down. Even the ghost towns are enjoying a population boom. Volcano, in the Mother Lode, which once had 10,000, is now up to 500.

Getting away from it all is getting to be the No. 1 problem in the No. 1 State. Chambers of commerce that used to crow, "Watch Us Grow!" are now thinking about posting "No Vacancy" signs, like motels on the weekend. There are Safeways in the redwoods and Rexalls in places so rustic they put cherries in the martinis. "Losing Population Fast!" will soon be the slogan that brings people running.

For San Franciscans it used to be simple. All they had to do was cross the bay to Marin and they were in what was called "the country," but there isn't much country left there or anywhere else. When the people in South San Mateo are out of sugar, they run across the street and borrow a cup from their neighbors in North Ventura. The wide open spaces are closing.

A place where time stood still. . . . This, along with peace and the abundant life, is part of the mid-twentieth-century dream. As the mindless freeways proliferate and the tract houses march across the hills like some monstrous toy gone mad, it suddenly becomes urgently important to find those unexploited reaches where the land still stretches wild and free, as far as the eye can see.

"This is the way it was before the spoilers came." Even a city man, geared to the dark streets between the walls he has built for himself, feels this primal urge to stand on headland or mountaintop and look at his own country through the eyes of those who came before him—to see it as they saw it. In California, time and the glorious land are running out. The Gold Rush has descended to its lowest level— The scramble for the almighty buck—and not even the redwoods are safe.

Time has not stood still, exactly, along the Mendocino coast, but its march has been unhurried and unruffled. On an April weekend, spring explodes in bursts of color across its meadows and hills and along its secret valleys, and there is scarcely a tourist or a neon sign to be seen in any direction.

There is a weather-beaten, almost Maine-like look to Mendocino. Beautiful old split fences zigzag across the fields. Horses run free among the grazing sheep. Ancient wagons, their iron tires rusting on lopsided wheels, stand in their old ruts alongside ramshackled farmhouses. You can travel for miles without seeing a stucco horror, and only in bustling Fort Bragg, dominated by the lordly stacks of Union Lumber, have the service stations and supermarkets gained a toehold.

It is a hidden world alive with ghosts—the ghosts of old lumber mills, the ghosts of wrecked lumber schooners, the ghosts of rumrunners who used Mendocino's dozens of coves and inlets during Prohibition. There are ghost towns that once counted their population in the thousands—roistering lumber towns where brothels and gambling houses flourished. Now you can see only the wooden churches with their crumbling steeples, and the silent streets that once were alive with the hard laughter of harlot and gambler.

But the true wonderland, in this lost enclave where the iris and the calla lilies grow wild, is Russian Gulch. Between Mendocino and Fort Bragg it is a moist, fern-filled valley that travels all the way back to the fables of childhood. Here, at last, is the enchanted forest of the fairy tales with its topless towers of redwood, its brook running clear over smooth pebbles glinting in the sun, its old wooden bridge where you can sit, legs dangling, and dream of the world as it might have been.

The trunks of giant redwoods, felled in a storm a century ago, lie head down in the water, their glistening flanks covered with the greenest moss. Here, amid the roar of the fall and the unearthly silence of trees that crashed unheard, you can hear at last the infinite voice of peace. It was a Saturday in the most restless state in the nation—and there was not another person in Russian Gulch.

As I drove back through the carpeted meadows, I had a vision of a developer standing on a hilltop, feasting his cold eyes on this unspoiled loveliness, and I shivered a little in the warm sun. Not too far down the road, around Timber Cove, the sheep are scrambling out of the way of the bulldozers. "One of these days," said a sharp young man, "we'll have another Russian River around here." He said it with pride. Nearby, a sheep said, "Baaaa." And I said, "Amen."

The sun was dying angrily behind the hills of Marin as we approached the thrusting towers of Baghdad-by-the-Bay. A black fog was roaring in over the skyline, and from the Embarcadero Freeway we could see the floodlit stacks of ships. With a happy shiver, we rolled up the windows and turned on the heater, pleased to be back in the cold embrace of the city that belongs only to itself.

California? A nice place to visit, but—

I admit it—I'm a native Californian who doesn't know his own state much better than the latest arrival from Waterloo, Iowa, and now that California is No. 1 in debts, taxes, and six-lane freeways, I'm getting a little sensitive about it.

I've fished for stripers with a throw-line in the Sacramento River, but I've never caught a salmon off the Gate. I've been to Las Vegas more often than I've visited Sutter's Mill, where gold was discovered by John Marshall or James Marshall, I'm never sure which. I've been ducking pigeons in Union Square for years, but I have yet to see the swallows return to Capistrano, and all I know about Highway 99 is that it's an odd number. I do know, however, that odd-numbered highways run north and south and even numbers east and west. That's not much, but it's something.

Of course, part of the trouble is that I live in San Francisco. When you live here, you're already there. I use "there" in the sense that Gertrude Stein used it when she was talking about Oakland; "The trouble with Oakland is that there's no *there* there." However, the late Gertrude is a little out of date too. There's much more *there* there than there ever was, but it's still not here, which is neither here nor there.

"It's very nice to go travelin'," as Frank Sinatra once sang, and I hope you all have a wonderful time—whoever and wherever you are: I'm glad your freeway was a safeway, may your sunburn be less than third degree, and good luck when you rejoin the bumper crop and head for chrome sweet home.

You fight the nits and gnats with loud cries of nutz, and I'll stay home, safely behind plate glass, and watch the Bay Bridge shoot golden Roman candles out over the bay. Good luck to you, sir, with your barbecue pit glowing like the rockets' red glare; your kid's rolling in the poison-oak patch again, and you're beginning to feel a little itchy yourself, aren't you? No hard feelings: you take the high road, and I'll take the city with the wall-to-wall pavement.

I don't mean to sound un-American. There's a lot to be said for getting away from it all even if you can't get away from yourself ("No matter where I go, I'm there too and spoil everything"). Lake Tahoe on a midsummer night is as enchanting as Lugano: the sky alight with stars as big as moons, the far-off whirring of a thousand slot machines, the midnight silence broken only by an occasional cry of "Bingo." The beaches from Stinson to Aptos to Laguna, a heavenly blend of suntan lotions, broken bottles and children cruising like sharks to kick sand in your face. If I have to have a beach, I'll take North Beach, where you can stroll slowly through the serfs and listen to the beat-beat-beat of the Beats as they pound against the walls of frustration.

The truth is that, like many a country boy before me, I respond to the city. I'm at home where the tall buildings grow, where the hustlers hustle and the busses bustle and the best way to climb a mountain is on a cable, clinging to an outside step and watching all those natural beauties teeter past on high heels. Give me a place where you can pick up a phone and call room service and have anything in the world delivered on a silver tray in 15 minutes flat, plus tip.

The concept of cities is changing. They are becoming horizontal, stretching out and out to infinite conformity or conforming infinity, villages laid end to end like cemeteries for the living. They're impossible to tell apart (the democracy of the mediocre)—one simple complex after another of supermarket-cum-super-bowling alley-cum-superdooper-burger shoppe, surrounding by a glittering forest of TV aerials atop look-alike houses populated by look-alike think-alikes. I'll take the vertical city, with its head in the clouds and its feet stuck solidly in concrete, surrounded by the wonderful, miserable clutter and jumble of the metropolis. It's a glorious mess, yet, but it's alive and kicking. Hard.

The city: how beautiful and ugly it is, unplanned, untamed, growing in and around itself because it has no place else to go. Improvising, compromising, fighting over every precious inch, going underground, chopping through hills, climbing over each other's shoulders, standing on tiptoe in an effort to see and be seen, peeking around corners, hanging onto cliffs with steel finger tips.

And yet, if it is a real city, it goes from one crisis to another with majesty, and emerges as a work of artless art: there is real felicity, for example, in the accidental grouping of the Russ and Shell Buildings, Mills Tower, Standard Oil, and Zellerbach—harmony in the discord of strong chords played with authority.

And the top of Nob Hill: no city planner, in his right (and rigid) mind, would think of juxtaposing the minaret'd Mark, the white granite Fairmont, and the brownstone effulgence of Bonanza Jim Flood, but there they are, in all their slapdash magnificence; Frank Lloyd Wright yelled "Wrong!" but it was he who didn't see that what is wrong is often more than Wright—in San Francisco.

The people are more honest, more sincere in the small towns? You've heard that, or something like that, all your lives. It may even be true, depending on your definition of honesty and sincerity. However, the city's characters are not without these qualities—plus the color and vitality that can exist only when hundreds of thousands, from a thousand different places, are thrown together on the crowded streets. There is everything in the city, right around the corner: from the excitement of an opening night to a fresh headline on the midnight editions to a rum drink with a gardenia in it.

The city: exciting, depressing, challenging, defeating, alive with noisy silences, reacting nervously to long-dead ghosts, frustrating, inspiring, moving maddeningly away the very moment you think you've discovered its pulse, ugly-beautiful, empty-overflowing, at once heartless and sentimental . . .

Well, why live in a city anyway? A hard life: the wall-to-wall pavement (accentuated by rachitic trees in concrete tubs), the constant conscience-prick of poverty amid wealth (pale cheek by fat jowl), the lip service and hypocrisy ("regardless of race, color, or creed"—and what is that menacing cry I hear just around the corner?), and the seemingly unresolvable questions of housing, inflation, traffic, jobs. And the taxes, always the taxes . . .

The city is in trouble, a trouble of its own making. The vital young move to the outskirts or the suburbs, preferring a bit of elbow room to the elbow in the ribs. They become commuters, choking the city by day, deserting it at night. Land becomes prohibitively high, the proliferating slums become profitable: the city belongs to the old rich and the eternal poor. The hospitals fill with the aged and indigent.

A fragmentation sets in, the tenuous cohesiveness is destroyed. The moneyed respectables withdraw to their well-prepared positions, portals guarded by doormen, and are afraid to venture out at night. The streets are filled with the alienated, wearing their strange raiment, flaunting the estrangement that is their common bond. The spired city, the sun glinting on its proud battlements, becomes an armed camp. Sirens scream at midnight, and the pockets of anger glow with banked fire.

This is the city, overwhelming, overwhelmed. I wouldn't live anywhere else.

What, then, is the allure, so often fatal? Perhaps it's something so simple as the knowledge that you're living in the mainstream, even if that mainstream at times becomes a raging torrent. For better or bitter, you are involved daily with the life of our times: there is no triumph or tragedy that does not affect you immediately and intimately.

In the city, you live among your peers—to be judged, weighed, measured by the harshest of standards: either you make it or you don't. If you do, there is no sweeter victory. If you don't, there is no more crushing defeat. Either way, you have fought the hardest fight on the most murderous terrain. The city is cruel, but gloriously and hideously alive, and that is the key word.

A great city lives. Its death throes are something to see. And the rattle in its throat is overwhelmingly loud, for the city dies no more easily than its struggling people. The battle is far from over.

There is a moment of truth for all cities, a time when it must stop in the midst of its mindless self-involvement and take a long, hard look at itself. Such a time has come for San Francisco, the pampered darling of American cities, the sacred enclave that lived so long beyond reality, head in the sky, feet on an extremely steep and, as it turns out, slippery hill.

San Francisco's Belle Époque—more properly, Cable Bell Époque—lasted from the Gold Rush days until the mid 1960s; in its Western brashness, even a disastrous earthquake was translated into a golden era. But in all truth, did any American city come so far so fast? Has any American city been so adorably precocious or extravagantly praised? Small wonder it has developed neurotic tendencies.

Thrice-blessed—dramatic hills, a great bay, a salubrious climate—San Francisco literally became world-famous overnight, the star story to end them all. Unknown Indian village into Spanish outpost—a mission, a presidio, church bells clashing with the wild cry of sea birds. A remote port of call on an almost unknown Western fringe, Indian canoes at dawn on a primeval bay, and then the cry of "Gold!" And San Francisco joined the list of magic cities.

The bay a sudden forest of masts. The Jasons came from everywhere. Great clippers rounded the Horn for the land of the golden fleecing, all canvas aloft and straining. San Francisco became an instant city with an instant past. As the wealth accumulated, mansions rose to house instantly great families, luxurious hotels appeared on the site of miners' tents, and there were restaurants, gambling halls, and bawdyhouses for every taste—all this in three roaring decades. No wonder San Franciscans were a cocky lot. And when the gold ran out, there were the silver mines of the Comstock Lode. Hail The Big Four and the bonanza kings, and soon their wives were importing clothes from Paris and flatware from London.

A unique city, young and yet cosmopolitan. By contrast, Los Angeles was what San Franciscans liked to describe as a sleepy Mexican village, if they thought about it at all. The contrast could not have been sharper. The San Francisco rich were already established in great banking houses, financing mining operations and thinking of opera seasons. The city was filled with restless adventurers from all over the world, creating a melting-pot atmosphere that exists to this day. Landlocked Los Angeles was growing slowly. Its people came overland, mainly from the Midwest and Southwest, drawn by the warm weather and the endless space.

This simple fact accounts for the startling differences between these two California cities—a few hundred miles apart geographically, a million miles apart in viewpoint and outlook. They could well be in different worlds.

"Ah, the touching arrogance of cities born only yesterday!"

An amused André Malraux, Minister of Culture of France, spoke thus after first hearing a San Franciscan refer to his city as "The Paris of the West."

But San Francisco is no more Paris, despite its chic and good French restaurants, than it is Naples, with its big Italian quarter, or Hong Kong, with its teeming, cluttered Chinatown. It is San Francisco, a city remarkable in itself. Eclectic, and yet with a character all its own. Tiny, as great cities go, and yet with the resources and energy for major efforts. Small in population—slowly decreasing, actually—but proud. Nevertheless, the storm warnings are everywhere.

San Francisco: a kaleidoscope in which the pieces no longer fall into place. The sweeping vistas are disappearing behind a Chinese wall of glass-backward highrises. The bay is being lost to sight and may someday be lost to posterity under a growing mountain of debris. The great old buildings, the palpable ties to the past of which the city was once so fond, disappear day by day in the sacred name of redevelopment and progress.

Mammon has always reigned upon some of the citied hills of San Francisco, but now his cold presence seems to be everywhere: from the tawdry commercialization of Chinatown and Fisherman's Wharf to the ticky-tacky building. The old rich, the so-called Establishment, is sitting more and more on its hands and money, meanwhile keeping the *nouveaux* at bay. The minorities, especially the Negro population (now one in ten in San Francisco, and growing), are speaking up, and the tone is unmistakable. North Beach, once the enchanted Little Italy of mamma-and-papa minestrone parlors and an invincible innocence, has become the headquarters of topless dancers and their cold-eyed promoters. Broadway, the heart of the section, is Bawdway, and even the post-bohemians have moved away, to the old sections near Golden Gate Park.

A changing city, but still a city, with all its joys and despair, its frustrations and accomplishments. The soiled and even tattered tapestry of metropolis continues to be marvelous to behold. In this small, infinitely precious area, such a richness of contrast, at once heart-warming and heart-shattering. Within a few blocks, glittering opera season and derelict with empty wine bottle, great ships from a dozen ports of hail and streetwalker loitering in Tenderloin doorway, soft voices in Pacific Heights drawing room and cry of rage at Hunters Point, a stupefying view from a Russian Hill penthouse and a family of seven in a Chinatown basement . . .

The problems of San Francisco are the problems of all great cities trapped in the turmoil and torment of mid-twentieth century. The only difference is that in San Francisco, you may still stand on a hilltop and feel the Pacific winds, cold and free. You can pause at a street corner and find the city spread out at your feet, bathed in a misty light that changes with each restless movement of the fog. A sea gull wheels overhead, a ship flying a strange flag moves distantly past, waves crash and boil at Land's End, and you feel again the surge of the San Franciscan: this can be—must be—the best of all possible cities.

The words are unspoken but strongly felt: there is yet time . . . there is yet time . . .

Well, I see I digressed, as usual. All I wanted to do was wish you happy traveling. And when you return, remember that the city waits for you as it waits for all its subjects: strongly alive, like a tiger on the hills, confident that nobody can really escape its endless fascinations.

LIST OF ILLUSTRATIONS

STRANGERS IN A CROWDED ROOM

THE EYE OF THE TOURIST

DONG KINGMAN loves his work. So do I, and thousands of others whose walls have been brightened and whose lives have been enriched by his artistry. But what I mean about Dong Kingman loving his work is this: in the thirty years that we have been friends, I have never seen him without his large notebook and India ink pen. As we chat in a Chinatown restaurant or walk the streets of Telegraph Hill, he is constantly sketching, sketching, sketching—in lightning, shorthand strokes that capture a landscape in a line, a likeness in a flash, a hidden corner that is suddenly illuminated and captured by the eternal freshness of his vision.

His friends call him Dong, but to himself, he is "Kingman." The phone will ring and there will be that chirpy voice: "Hello, this is Kingman." The phone rings quite often, for although Dong lives in Manhattan, just around the corner from the Plaza Hotel, he is constantly on the move. To San Francisco. To Hong Kong, Hollywood, Europe—and always with his big notebook and busy pen, recording the wonderful world of Kingman, a happy world of bright scenes and hopeful people.

In his artistic outlook, he is only being true to himself, for Dong is one of the happiest people I know. His bright eyes dance, he speaks in chuckles, and he seems never to be bored, the true mark of the person who is not a bore. I have never asked him his age, for he shows no signs of any. He must be somewhere between fifty or sixty, but he still seems as young, trim, and bouncy as the day I met him, in 1936. At that time, he was painting for the WPA, and even then, knowledgeable San Franciscans were buying Kingmans as fast as he painted them.

Today, the fame of this dapper little man—he must be the best-dressed of artists—is established and secure. He is represented in the permanent collections of the country's leading museums and universities—among them the Metropolitan Museum, Whitney Museum, American Academy of Arts and Letters, Museum of Modern Art, Boston Museum, Art Institute of Chicago, and the San Francisco Museum. His awards include two Guggenheim fellowships, the $500 first award of the Metropolitan Museum in 1953, both the Philadelphia Watercolor Prize and the Pennell medal at the Pennsylvania Academy, three prizes of the American Watercolor Society Annuals, and the Audubon Gold Medal of Honor.

Born in California, educated in Hong Kong, an important figure in the life of New York, Dong Kingman is still very much a San Franciscan at heart, for that city first recognized his talent. Shortly after he moved to New York, I visited him at his studio, where I found him by a window, painting a row of trees. Looking out the window and seeing only rooftops, I asked, "Where do you see those trees?"

"In Portsmouth Square in San Francisco," he said, grinning.

And it occurred to me then, as it does now, that no matter where or what he paints, there will always be something of San Francisco in the art of Dong Kingman, as this book so eloquently attests.

HERB CAEN

190

Herb Caen
by Doug Knitzman

A NOTE ON THE BOOK

This book was set in the monophoto version of Bembo. The original face was cut by Francesco Griffo for the Venetian printer Aldus Manutius and first used in Cardinal Bembo's *De Aetna*, 1495, hence the name of the contemporary version. The layout, typography, and binding design were done by Joseph P. Ascherl with Elsa Anderson.